The Pastorals and Polycarp

PUBLISHED VOLUMES

Vol. 1: The Gospel of Mark, DARYL D. SCHMIDT

Vol. 2: The Infancy Gospels of James and Thomas, RONALD F. HOCK

Vol. 3: The Gospel of Matthew, ROBERT T. FORTNA

Vol. 4: The Gospel of Luke, RICHARD I. PERVO

Vol. 5: The Pastorals and Polycarp, RICHARD I. PERVO

The Pastorals and Polycarp

TITUS, 1–2 TIMOTHY, AND POLYCARP TO THE PHILIPPIANS

The Scholars Bible

RICHARD I. PERVO

Annotated with Introduction

POLEBRIDGE PRESS
Salem, Oregon

Cover image: Fresco representing St. Polycarp from the Ravanica monastery (1375–1377) in the Kučaj mountains near Ćuprija in Central Serbia. Photo compliments of the Steven Enich Serbian Orthodox Church Cultural Collection, Hilandar Research Library, The Ohio State University. Used by permission.

Cover and interior design by Robaire Ream

Polebridge Press is the publishing arm of the Westar Institute, a non-profit, public-benefit research and educational organization. To learn more, visit westarinstitute.org.

Library of Congress Cataloging-in-Publication Data

Names: Pervo, Richard I., author. | Polycarp, Saint, Bishop of Smyrna. Epistola ad Philippenses. English.
Title: The Pastorals and Polycarp : Titus, 1-2 Timothy, and Polycarp to the Philippians / by Richard I. Pervo.
Other titles: Bible. Pastoral epistles English. Scholars. 2016. | Bible. Pastoral epistles. Greek. 2016.
Description: Salem : Polebridge Press, 2016. | Series: The scholars Bible | Includes bibliographical references and index.
Identifiers: LCCN 2016023549 | ISBN 9781598151787 (alk. paper)
Subjects: LCSH: Bible. Pastoral epistles--Criticism, interpretation, etc. | Polycarp, Saint, Bishop of Smyrna. Epistola ad Philippenses.
Classification: LCC BS2735.52 .P47 2016 | DDC 227/.8305209--dc23
LC record available at https://lccn.loc.gov/2016023549

10 9 8 7 6 5 4 3 2 1

CONTENTS

PREFACE

"Scholars Bible" means "by scholars" rather than "primarily for scholars." The series attempts to provide accessible introductions and comments to accompany fresh and vivid translations, with original texts for those who have some Greek. This, a continuation of work on the Pauline legacy, is the first of two projected volumes, to be followed by a contribution on Colossians, Ephesians, and 2 Thessalonians.

Because the Scholars Bible is not limited by canonical boundaries, it is possible to place in juxtaposition two works with some striking similarities: the Pastoral Epistles and Polycarp's letter to the Philippians. Their appearance under a single cover will be of value and interest to a range of readers. Once the debate over authorship, which has introduced almost nothing fresh for over a generation, has been abandoned, the possibility of looking at the Pastorals as literature and examination of other fictitious letter collections arises. This little book engages in some of that work and points those interested toward other resources. I am entirely responsible for the translation.

As always, thanks are due to the patient, diligent, and creative staff of Polebridge Press.

Richard I. Pervo
Saint Paul, Minnesota

ABBREVIATIONS

AcPaul	Acts of Paul
Cels.	Origen, *Contra Celsum* (*Against Celsus*)
1,2 Clem	1,2 Clement
Col	Colossians
1,2 Cor	1,2 Corinthians
Eph	Ephesians
Exod	Exodus
Gal	Galatians
Haer.	Irenaeus, *Adversus haereses* (*Against Heresies*)
Heb	Hebrews
Hist. eccl.	Eusebius, *Historia ecclesiastica* (*Ecclesiastical History*)
IgnMag	Ignatius to the Magnesians
IgnSm	Ignatius to the Smyrnaeans
IgnTr	Ignatius to the Trallians
IgnPol	Ignatius to Polycarp
Jas	James
Matt	Matthew
ms(s)	manuscript(s)
NT	New Testament
OT	Old Testament
PE	Pastoral Epistles
1,2 Pet	1,2 Peter
Phil	Philippians
Phlm	Philemon
PolPhil	Polycarp to the Philippians
Rom	Romans
1,2 Thess	1,2 Thessalonians
1,2 Tim	1,2 Timothy
Tob	Tobit
v(v).	verse(s)

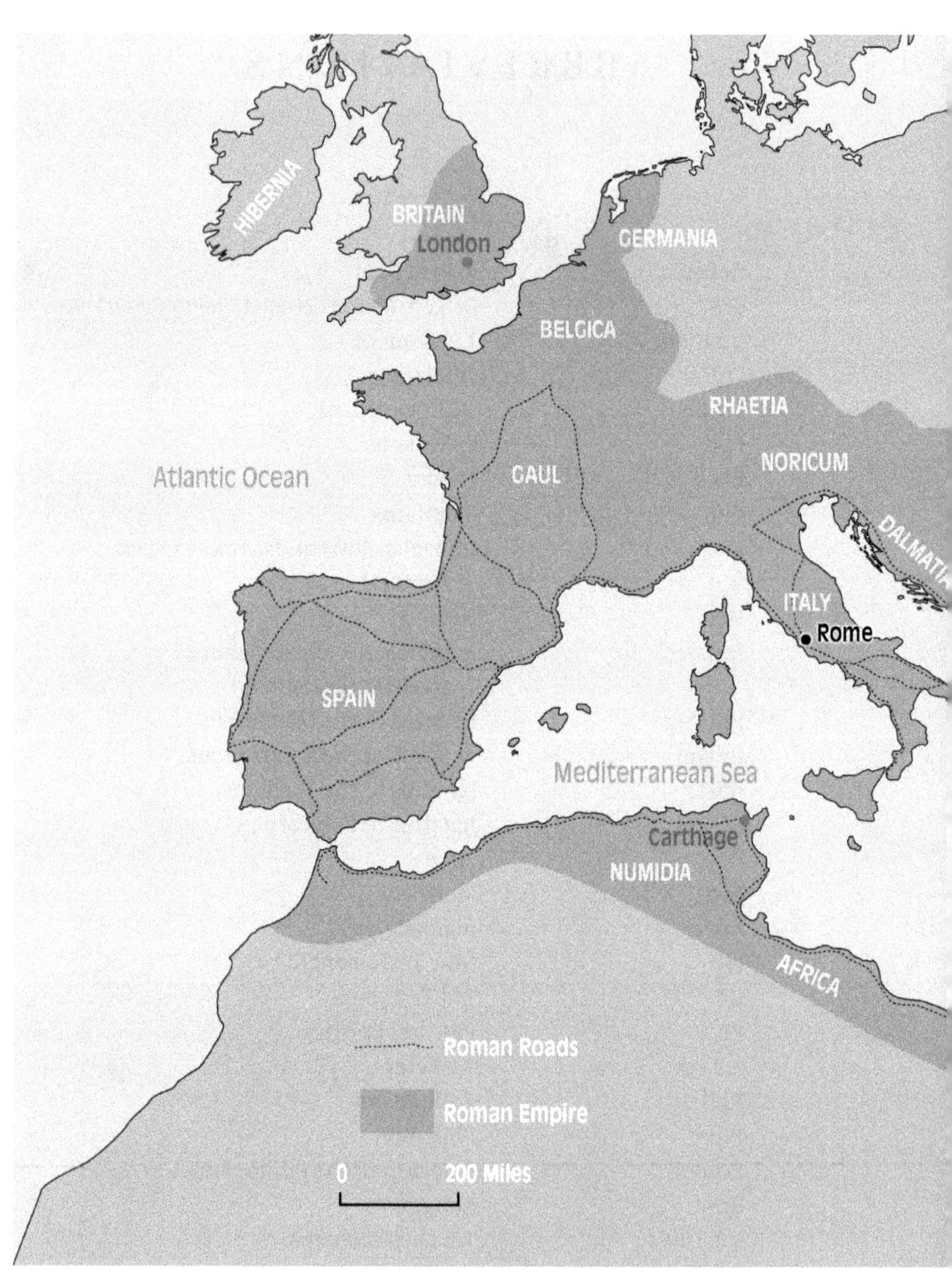

The Roman Empire in the First Century.

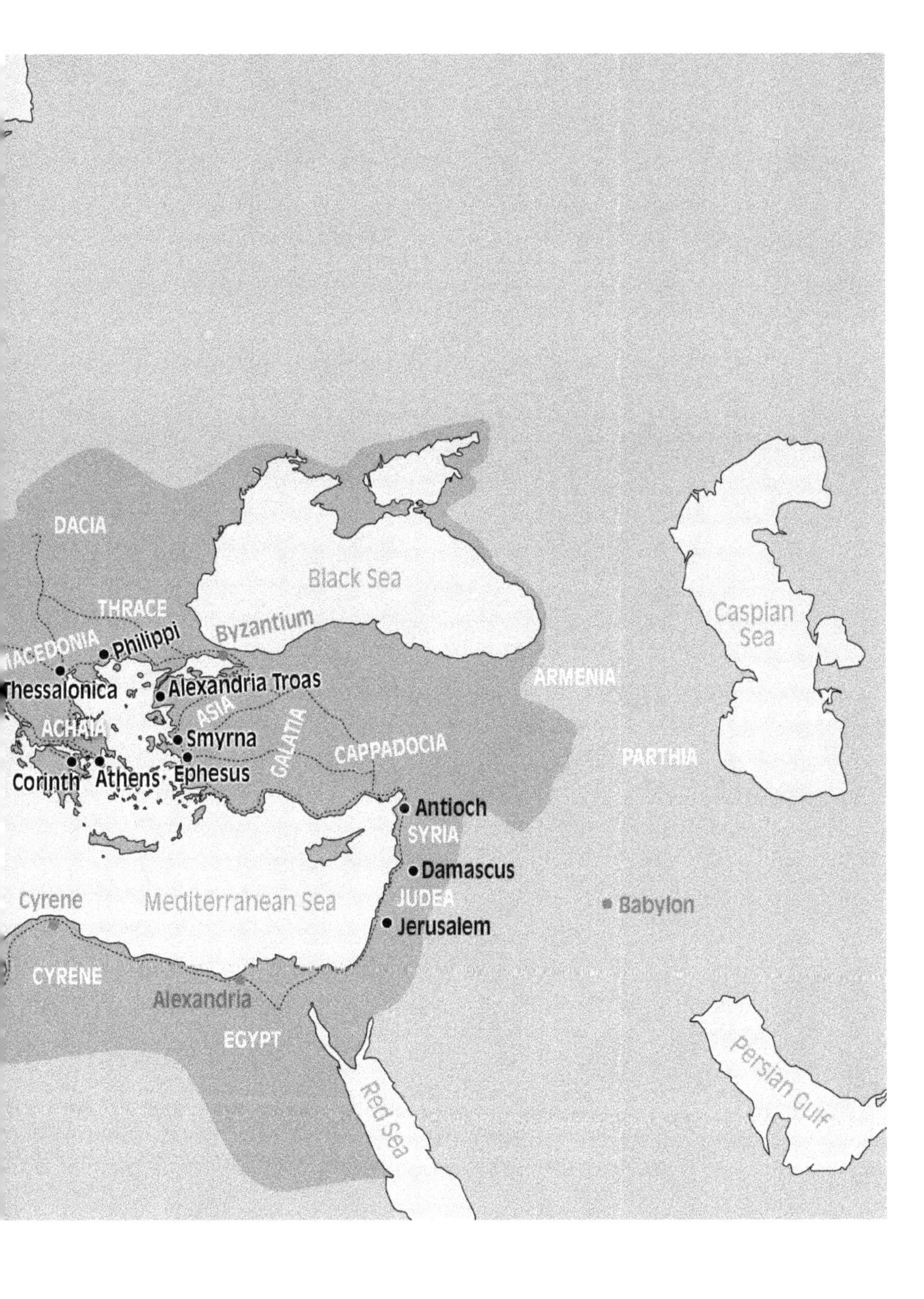

DACIA
Black Sea
THRACE
Byzantium
ACEDONIA
Philippi
Thessalonica
Alexandria Troas
ASIA
ACHAIA
Smyrna
GALATIA
CAPPADOCIA
Corinth
Athens
Ephesus
ARMENIA
Caspian Sea
PARTHIA
Antioch
SYRIA
Damascus
Cyrene
Mediterranean Sea
JUDEA
Jerusalem
Babylon
CYRENE
Alexandria
EGYPT
Red Sea
Persian Gulf

THE PASTORALS

INTRODUCTION

1. Ephesus, Provenance

Ephesus, approximately in the middle of the west coast of Asia Minor, was an old Ionian city, evidence for which goes back to c. 900 BCE. After various vicissitudes Ephesus expanded during the Hellenistic period and became, under Rome, the provincial capital and metropolis. Ephesus was a major center of Paul's missionary activity and probably his greatest success. Other early followers of Jesus also labored and battled there, making Ephesus the place best attested in early Christian history. There Paul's letters were quite probably first collected, edited, and published. At Ephesus, Colossians, Ephesians, (possibly) 2 Thessalonians, Luke/Acts, and the Pastoral Epistles (PE) were composed. Outside of the direct Pauline sphere were Revelation and 1–3 John. Ignatius wrote a lengthy letter to Ephesus. The apologist Justin Martyr was long associated with the metropolis.[1]

The city also witnessed the climax of several Pauline trajectories. The speculative, wisdom trend visible in 1 Corinthians, where Paul seeks to throw some cold water on the blaze he had kindled, erupts in Colossians and is deflected by Ephesians. The friendly pastoral letter represented by 1 Thessalonians and Philippians gives way to the more formal and less friendly pastoral direction represented by the PE. Paul's dialectical mode of argumentation (Romans, 1 Corinthians, Galatians) is implicitly rejected by the PE, which call for giving opponents the silent treatment.

Unity within particular communities and among various communities is prominent in Romans, potent in Ephesians, embraced by Luke and Acts, enshrined by the PE, and preached by Polycarp and Ignatius, becomes a stable and enduring theme. One of the questions raised by the Pauline tradition that remains vital for groups of every sort is the depth and nature of the prices to be paid for unity. The PE manifest a decisive shift away from the

1. For a detailed bibliography see Pervo, "Acts in Ephesus (and Environs) c. 115." Trebilco, *The Early Christians in Ephesus*, provides a broad and judicious survey. Note the varied essays in Koester, *Ephesos*.

Pauline model of unity amidst diversity. Regrettable as this may be to many, the historian's task is to explore why and how the changes occurred.

2. Text, Style

Although the existence of the PE is certain from c. 135 (see Reception and Influence below), the extant text belongs to the fourth century and later. But one early papyrus, 𝔓[32] (early third century), with parts of a few verses of Titus has been identified. The PE were not included in 𝔓[46], the early third-century edition of the Pauline corpus. Codex Vaticanus (B), one of the great fourth-century bibles, lacks the PE because the latter part of the NT is lost. Data suffice to indicate the existence of a D-Text ("Western") edition, although many of its variants are minor or pedantic.

Stylistic questions have long been in thrall to the question of authorship. Striking to any reader is the percentage of *hapaxes*, words found only in the PE. A good 37 percent of the vocabulary fits this character. One third of the words used in the PE are not found in the undisputed letters of Paul. A number of these do not appear in Christian writings before the second century. Quantitative analyses can always generate debate, but the difference between the Pastorals and undisputed Paulines cannot be obscured.[2] Absent from the PE are such central Pauline terms as *free/freedom*, *circumcision*, *apocalypse*, *testament*, *righteousness of God*, *body of Christ*, *abound*, and *boast*.

The style of these letters is often criticized for its lack of Pauline vigor, logic, and developed argumentation.[3] The different styles reflect different eras. Paul wrote at the dynamic and experimental beginning of a movement. The Pastor's style reflects his values: order, stability, and conventionality. More can be said. If the Pastor is no poet, he has a good ear, as is shown by his use of

2. Harrison's studies in *Problem* and *Paulines* remain impressive.
3. See Nigel Turner's survey, *Style*, 101–5.

Why the "Pastoral Epistles"?

Thomas Aquinas characterized 1 Timothy as a rule for pastors. The specific title is traced to Paul Anton in 1726 and has been employed since then. The term recognizes that these epistles do not pertain to the early days of the Pauline mission, but to the needs of established communities. In the second and later centuries Paul was viewed primarily as a pastor, rather than a missionary.

liturgical/creedal passages (e.g., 1 Tim 2:5–6; 3:16; 6:13–16; 2 Tim 1:9–10; 2:11–13; Titus 3:4–7). This author is sparing in his use of imagery, but those selected are apt and memorable, as in 2 Tim 2:4–7. The ringing triplet of 2 Tim 4:7 has attained familiarity for many to whom the Bible is not a familiar book. This leads to a kindred observation: 2 Timothy represents a sensitive use of pathos, so powerful that people do not wish to deprive Paul of its authorship. At their best the PE offer a stately and sonorous prose, not unlike that of the tradition of *The Book of Common Prayer* (the early editions of which borrowed freely from the Pastorals).

3. Genre, Structure, Order

These three short letters display a complex overall picture. This reflects the relevance of the Pauline letters to communities, administrative correspondence, literature about organizations, popular philosophical advice, testaments (the last words of dying persons), and fiction. The PE follow the form of Pauline correspondence but differ in that the ostensible addressees are individuals rather than communities.[4] Since the addressees are leaders, 1–2 Timothy have some of the official character of instructions from superiors to subordinates.

In so far as these instructions about behavior apply to community members in general, they are indebted to the popular philosophical tradition, which sought to inculcate upper-class men with suitable ethical standards.[5] This contrast is readily overlooked: early Christians sought to teach people of quite modest status, at best, standards intended for their "betters." For us the Pastor's list of qualifications for leaders sets the bar distressingly low. This misses the point: The Pastor's object was to spread the message that Christians were ordinary members of society, staunch supporters of the social order. If someone were to look at the Pastor's qualifications for bishops and say, "How utterly conventional," that worthy gentleman would reply: "Thank you."[6]

Consonant with these goals is the inclusion of two genres: the Household Code and the Church Order. The former of these emerged in the

4. Philemon is addressed to "Philemon our dear friend and co-worker, to Apphia our sister, to Archippus our fellow soldier, and to the church in your house."

5. General readers will find many references to popular philosophy in the commentary of Fiore, *The Pastoral Epistles*.

6. For a striking illustration, see Onosander's list of the qualities of a general, appendix 3 in Dibelius and Conzelmann, *The Pastoral Epistles*, 158–60. Many of these would be no less suitable for any profession.

Deuteropauline tradition (Col 3:18–4:1; Eph 5:22–6:9; 1 Pet 2:18–3:7), utilizing three traditional household pairs: husbands/wives, parents/children, and owners/slaves as a basis for family values. The PE blend this type with the emerging Church Order. Elements of the Church Order can be seen in Matthew 18 and Jas 5:12–19. The earliest free-standing example is the *Didachē*. The PE share this combination with only one other text: Polycarp to the Philippians. For the Pastor the rationale is clear: his ecclesiology views the church as the household of faith.

2 Timothy is strongly indebted to the Testament genre, which had deep and widespread roots, from Plato's dialogues about Socrates' last days to the farewell address of Joseph found in Genesis 48–50. The genre flourished in

The Pauline Letter

Letters are substitutes for personal conversation. Antiquity witnessed many types of correspondence. Paul's letters are more like official missives than notes to friends. They reflect the utilization of many forms and types. Attention to formal features helps interpretation and can be of considerable use in determining questions of authenticity and integrity. The following is a standard outline with references to Romans as examples.

Opening

1:1	a. Sender
1:7	b. Addressee
	c. Greeting
1:8–17	d. Thanksgiving

Body

1:13–8:39	a. Formal Opening
	b. Text
8:31–39	c. Eschatological Close
15:14–33	d. Parousia/Travel Plans

Paraenesis

12:1–15:13

Closing

16:3–23

a. Greetings from Others
b. Doxology
c. Blessing (15:33)

Second Temple Judaism, as in the Testaments of the Twelve Patriarchs. The Jewish testaments abounded in ethical exhortation and utilized personal example, as well as novelistic features. Paul's farewell to the presbyters of Ephesus (Acts 20:17–38) offers many close correspondences to the PE, for which it may have been an inspiration. Use of the Testament style transports the PE into the realm of literature. That generates hypotheses argued for in the following paragraphs.

Firstly, the PE are a collection, a group intended to be read as such. One may reasonably ask why the Pastor did not compose a single letter. Squeezing out the repetition and redundancy, he could have produced an epistle of about ten chapters. Reasons for producing a group will emerge in the ensuing discussion. The order of the collection is important. The canonical order is based upon length, from longest to shortest, as well as grouping the letters to Timothy together, but this order should not be taken at face value. 2 Timothy is quite apparently the final item. The order of the other two is debatable; I propose Titus, 1 Timothy, 2 Timothy. Support for this comes from the structure: Titus, the shortest piece, has the longest epistolary opening, while 2 Timothy has the longest closing. Although comparison to fictitious letter collections is appropriate (below), the PE probably assume an edition of Paul's letters.[7]

A second proposition is that the PE relate a story or stories, that is, they have narrative as well as thematic coherence. Epistolary narratives are rarely sequential. Readers must often engage in some labor to piece out the sequence provided and presumed by various bits and pieces, and must fill in gaps, as well. Characterization is another literary feature of the PE. The text is accessorized with minor characters, about whom readers wish to learn more and who may reappear and otherwise fit into the broader story. Among them are opponents, who, contrary to the tradition, are identified. Some names recur, such as Hymenaeus (1 Tim 1:20; 2 Tim 2:17) and Alexander (1 Tim 1:20; 2 Tim 4:14). We should like to know what harm Alexander the coppersmith did to Paul. On the other side is Onesiphorus and family, richly evoked (2 Tim 1:16–18; 4:19). In 2 Timothy 4 the demands of pathos and the desire to provide a supportive entourage collide: After lamenting that Luke alone remains with him, Paul goes on to mention three others who send greetings. As much as the Pastor worries about women, he does not name any of those regarded as enemies. Although it was customary not to mention the names of living women, the ubiquitous Prisca receives a greeting in 2 Tim 4:19.

7. Alfred Barnett, *Paul Becomes a Literary Influence*, concludes that "the author of the Pastorals was acquainted with Paul's letters as a collection and that he knew each of the ten letters" (277). Others are less generous, but wide acquaintance is accepted.

Major characters are Paul, Titus, and Timothy. The latter two are young (Titus 2:7, 15b; 1 Tim 4:12) and utterly devoid of experience, competence, and discernible intelligence. The advantage of this is that the Pastor can convey basic instruction to them—and thus to those peeking over their shoulders. Titus, like Paul, once led a sinful life (Titus 3:4–5; 1 Tim 1:12–17), whereas Timothy can look back to generations of faithful forebears, as can Paul (2 Tim 1:3–14; 3:15).

Their roles are managerial, involving limited authority and considerable responsibility. Titus' sphere is that of a "new mission field," Crete, whereas Timothy serves the well-established metropolis of Ephesus. False teachers are nonetheless a problem for each (Titus 1:10–16; 3:8–11). For Titus rivals are outsiders; members of the community plague Timothy. Unlike Paul's polemics, which engage those who disagree with his theological positions, in the PE opponents are in conflict with the *tradition*. In sum, the PE show how leaders of a now defined movement are to deal with a variety of situations by employing their different gifts.

The chief character is Paul, who rose from being a vicious enemy of Jesus' followers and essentially a "pagan" to becoming a great and suffering apostle to all. 1 Timothy and Titus do not imply a "late" setting in the life of Paul. Paul is engaged in his great missionary labors in the Aegean region, what has been called the "Third Missionary Journey." Outside of winter, when travel was avoided, the apostle is constantly in motion. 2 Timothy brings a new and unexplained situation. Paul is incarcerated and being tried at Rome, on unstated charges that will lead to his execution. Once more, readers are compelled to fill in narrative gaps.

Similar observations may be made about the abundance of personal references in the PE, which surpass those of the church letters in detail and frequency. Their verisimilitude lent strength to the claim of Pauline authorship and an interim theory that the Pastor made use of a number of authentic fragments.[8] This was a categorical error. When the PE are studied alongside fictions of the same era, the author's need for adherence to some conventions of realism (which vary in literary cultures) and the quest for verisimilitude are immediately apparent. The fictional character of the PE emerges in a manner that would make a literary editor wince. At Titus 3:12, after detailed instructions for setting up and taking charge of communities on Crete, Titus is abruptly told to drop everything and hasten to Paul's winter quarters. All of the personal details are decorations for the timeless content of the church order.

8. So Harrison, *Problem*. He later abandoned that position.

Relevant comparative material exists. Greco-Roman antiquity saw the productions of numerous collections of letters attributed to a famous figure. One such collection formed a nucleus of the Alexander-Romance. In these the dutiful son wrote home to Mom about the wonders he witnessed. The great majority of these collections deal with the subject's legacy and with the preservation of the movement. Not all are fictional. The letters of Plato, a major impetus for the practice of pseudonymous collections, are comprised of thirteen items, some of which are generally viewed as authentic. The Pauline corpus provides an interesting parallel. Advice to statesmen plays a prominent role in the Platonic collection, comparable to the directions for church leaders in the PE. Five letters attributed to Euripides provide a guide for rulers. Aeschines wrote twelve epistles in exile; politics are the major theme. Two dozen letters of Hippocrates extol Democritus. Chion (seventeen) is a collection that meets modern criteria for an epistolary novel. Philosophical justification of tyrannicide is the theme. The twenty-one letters of Themistocles provide a psychological study. Establishment of the Socratic legacy is a guiding theme of the thirty-five items in the relevant corpus. All of these examples present their material in chronological order.[9]

Study of these collections and epistolary novels is highly illuminating for the PE. They represent the same intersection of popular philosophy, establishment and maintenance of a legacy, and literary fiction. Recognition of the affinity with epistolary novels removes the PE from mere, often unfavorable, comparison with the church letters and offers suggestions for the question of why this small collection of short letters rather than one full-size treatise on community organization and by-laws. One could write a commentary on the PE drawing entirely upon epistolary novels for both the intellectual and the literary background.

The comparative task has benefitted from the work of Timo Glaser, who, sparked by an exploratory probe, developed a dissertation later issued as a monograph.[10] Here readers will find many rich insights and penetrating observations gleaned from epistolary novels. When scholars can finally move beyond the discussion of authenticity and look at the PE as they are, these texts will be of great utility for illuminating the intellectual and literary world of the instructions to Timothy and Titus.

9. An epistolary novel based upon contributions from the Seven Sages probably existed, and embedded within the voluminous correspondence of Phalaris is another example of the genre. See Holzberg, *Der griechische*, and "Letters: *Chion*."

10. The probe was Pervo, "Romancing." The monograph is Glaser, *Paulus*.

This section closes with a sample from Cynic Epistles 21, which shows the familiar combination of personal details with exhortations to preserve the master's legacy.

> Aeschines to Xanthippe, the Wife of Socrates. (1) I gave Euphro of Megara six measures of barley meal and eight drachmas and a new coat for you. . . . Remember what Socrates used to say and try to follow his customs and advice. . . . (3) So, take courage, Xanthippe, and do not discard any of the good instructions of Socrates.[11]

4. Occasion, Circumstances, Social World, Rival Teaching

General rather than specific circumstances appear to have motivated the Pastor. The irruption of rival teaching is not a likely immediate cause, for the Pastor neither provides a very clear profile of the view or views opposed nor supplies counter arguments. He does not argue that moral anarchy threatens, against which a firm structure must be erected. One difficulty is that innovation is suspect. If the author wishes to recommend some fresh solutions, they must be characterized as traditional.

No less improbable would be the contention that the author wishes to rescue the apostle from the clutches of naughty heretics, who have appropriated his thought and brought his name into utter disrepute. The author assumes that Paul enjoys high status among his potential audience. The PE belong to the contentions about the Pauline legacy. All who sought to preserve Paul's contribution engaged in reinterpretation. The PE will strike many as the most deviant representative of that effort in the New Testament (NT). Nevertheless, the Pauline roots of the Pastor's values deserve recognition. As noted above, for the Pastor the primary expression of Paul's desire for unity was through uniformity. The apostle did not rejoice in rather uninhibited social experimentation, although its grounds lay in his own teaching (1 Corinthians). He cared about what outsiders thought (e.g. 1 Thess 4:12). For the Pastor outsiders *must* think well of the Christian community. The outsiders he has in mind are not freed up free-spirited advocates of social pluralism. They are staunch defenders of traditional families, traditional values, and the tried and true. Members of contemporary Western societies view their societies as always evolving and argue over how rapid and profound change should be and what is baby, what bath water. Both liberals and conservatives strive to identify the core.

11. Trans. Malherbe, *The Cynic Epistles*, 371.

For much of the world today and all of it in the second century, society was viewed as a stable order derived from or at least consonant with nature, and the whole thing ordained by the divine. The Pastor did not wonder if slavery was impermanent, or if the day would come when families headed by a dominant father were no longer the norm. In short, rather than turning the world upside down and shaking it, the gospel reinforces the social order. A useful, if potentially superficial, contrast is that for Paul the world was ephemeral and not worth much effort: paper plates should not be preserved like bone china. The Pastor regards contemporary family values as sterling.

For the Pastor society was here to stay; big problems awaited those who picked fights with it. Persecution was a real threat. The Pastor does not pretend otherwise, but he does not want superheroes like the Paul of Acts, and no one needs to make the case for his strong distaste for superheroines, such as Thecla. He has read Acts 13–14, from which he draws only notices of persecutions. The Pastor's model is unlike that which would long dominate Christendom. "Focus on the family" would be an apt motto: closely knit family units that stressed moderation rather than extremes, social conformity rather than deviation, life that subordinated individual views to family interests.

The norm is the patriarchal family. The possibility of families headed by widows or divorcées does not merit consideration. If this seems improbable, American families of the 1950s envisioned by the media and popular culture were of the same type. Father *should* know best, even if he sometimes erred. Women's official authority was limited to the home. Yet even the kindest and most generous critics of the PE will have to concede that the author has problems with women. Data to dissect the Pastor's psyche are largely lacking; what we do have is chapters 3–4 of the Acts of Paul. Thecla embodies everything about women against which the Pastor warns us. She is independent, rebellious, contemptuous of imperial authority, aggressively celibate, a missionary willing to bob her hair and wear men's attire—in fact she plays her most dangerous scenes naked, a state unlikely to enhance family honor then or in later ages. However one construes this conflict, it reveals two ecclesial and theological models.[12]

The canonical Deuteropauline texts show successive retrenchment on female emancipation, a trajectory that Paul is already blunting in 1 Corinthians. For the Pastor such behavior presents the church as a subversive organization. Were he to concede the validity of equality in Christ but urge prudence and restraint as a current tactic, this author might command a

12. See MacDonald, *The Legend and the Apostle*, who views 1 Timothy and the Acts of Paul as intentionally opposing texts and stories.

modicum of sympathy. Instead he inscribes the patriarchal household into the divine order of the universe.[13] Moreover, he never talks to—let alone listens to—women. Instead, he talks about them. The Pastor's misogyny has one social and a two-fold theological grounding, both interrelated. He is committed to supporting the patriarchal model of the household as the microcosm of city and empire; he desires to distance the church from any taint of threat to the social order; and he evidently holds women responsible for some of the teaching he opposes.

When you plant a radish, you get a radish, not a Brussel sprout. Good teaching produces good fruit, that is, patriarchy-embracing households filled with silent, obedient women, decorous children, and abject slaves. Sound doctrine, to utilize one of the Pastor's favorite metaphors, produces sound communities. Unsound doctrine has, alas, not yet become extinct. Opposition to rival teaching is not, to reiterate, the author's primary purpose. The Pauline tradition came to deem it wise to give some attention to opposing viewpoints in every text. Acts 20 envisions wolves falling upon Paul's little lambs. Romans 16:17–20 is an interpolation crafted to fit the polemical menu. Colossians is a friendly letter containing a polemical passage. Considered as a conflated text, Philippians is friendly correspondence with an inserted attack upon rivals. Rival teaching is a problem for the Pastor, but not *the* problem. Indeed, he seeks to use the presence of opponents to strengthen his case.

The method for combatting opponents involves, at most, telling them that they are wrong and declining further dialogue. One is strongly tempted to suspect that the Pastor lacks the material and the ability needed to win such arguments. (It was not until the era of the Apologists, from c. 150 onward, that theologians in what would become the mainstream tradition acquired the skills and tools needed to refute their opponents on intellectual grounds.) Coupled with the refusal of dialogue is a tendency to invoke the stereotypes of character assassination to disqualify rivals. At 2 Tim 3:6 the Pastor can join two prejudices by referring to "silly women" ("stupid bimbos" in current slang) as the harvest gleaned by his rivals.

A venerable approach is to list all the views opposed and construct a profile of the opponents, preferably one known from other sources. This is not a desirable approach here, for the Pastor appears to identify a number of views found suspect. Some could be related to a "Judaizing" Christian movement as seen in topics like Law (1 Tim 1:7) and Jewish adversaries (Titus 1:10), but the issue of food may be related to an ascetic orientation (Titus 1:15),

13. As late as 1899, J. H. Bernard says, à propos of 1 Tim 6:2: "Equal membership in the Kingdom of Christ is not to be a pretext for the neglect of social duty to superiors."

as is prohibition of marriage (1 Tim 4:7). Speculation is not recommended (1 Tim 6:3–5), quite probably represented in the interest in "myths and genealogies" (1 Tim 1:1–7). 2 Timothy 2:18 speaks of realized eschatology. Judging from what can be inferred from Revelation and other sources, it is highly probable that one or more forms of Pauline speculation in Ephesus and its environs troubled the Pastor, and that such ideas were associated with freedom from worldly conventions. "Judaizing" communities presented an anti-Pauline viewpoint. Paulinist movements would be both outside in that their proponents dominated some house-based communities and inside in so far as they had appeal for some persons associated with the Pastor.[14] The accusation that greed motivated the opponents was already hoary with age, but the Pastor is no less concerned about its corrosive effects upon his loyal followers (as was Polycarp).

5. Sources, Intertextuality

As indicated above, the Pastor knows a collection of Pauline letters. He cites the Gospel of Luke (1 Tim 5:18), and evidently knows Acts, as 2 Tim 3:11 suggests: "The sufferings experienced in Pisidian Antioch, Iconium, and Lystra! The persecutions I endured there! But the master delivered me from all of them." On the grounds that Acts 13–14 are essentially Lucan composition rather than a reflection of a detailed source, 2 Timothy shows Luke's editorial work in Acts, as that book reports persecutions in Antioch, Iconium, and Lystra, in that order, but not at Derbe. The existence of a parallel source with the same structure is rather improbable.[15]

The Christological hymnic passages were developed in Pauline circles on the basis of Hellenistic Jewish models. Some or all of the "gospel truth" sayings (1 Tim 1:15; 3:1; 4:9; 2 Tim 2:11; Titus 3:8) probably derive from tradition, as may other short items, but no longer are the sources evident.

Despite the well-known sonority of 2 Tim 3:15–16, the LXX plays no major role. 2 Tim 2:19 looks like a citation, but neither sentence reflects a single LXX text. The sole case where a Pauline citation formula is used, 1 Tim 5:18, the citations come from 1 Cor 9:9 and Luke 10:7. Whatever the value of the Old Testament (OT), it appears to be of more use to the Pastor's opponents than to the sound instruction (Titus 1:14–15; 1 Tim 1:4).

14. See Trebilco, *The Early Christians in Ephesus*, 209–35, for a detailed study that seeks to locate the PE in the final quarter of the first century. Pervo, "Acts in Ephesus (and Environs) c. 115," argues that the data better fit the circumstances of a generation later.

15. See Pervo, *Acts*, 319–21.

6. Theology

The Pastor presents a developed or evolved Paulinism responsive to several factors.[16] In terms of method, dialogue and argumentation have been discontinued. Resort to speculation grounded in the Wisdom tradition has been left to opponents. With regard to presuppositions, the eschatological tension that provided a framework for Paul has lost its force. To refer to the "Delay of the Parousia" (end-time) is no more than a half truth. Believers live between two Advents, in a period of indefinite length. The Pastor has replaced the term *parousia* (coming, arrival) with "epiphany." The latter has a wider and more flexible range of meaning in ancient religion. Salvation, the receipt of eternal life, is the primary goal of Christian existence. While reaffirming the traditional Pauline formula of salvation by faith apart from human action, the Pastor regards good works as a necessary compliment to salvation. All of these factors are logical outcomes of changed circumstances. Quite distinct from Paul is the view of unity brought about by salvation. The Pastor sees salvation as a product of obedience to community rulers and the principles they espouse. The ship of the church is launched on a course that will bring the winds of nature and the currents of grace into harmony, if not identity.

The invisible God becomes apparent in the epiphany of Christ, mediator between natural and supernatural worlds—mediator and judge. These roles reflect two epiphanies, the first as human agent of God, the second as judge. The vocabulary for this epiphany Christology was supplied by the earlier Hellenistic and contemporary Roman ruler cults, which had learned how to depict a human representative of divine transcendence without the temporal apparatus utilized by apocalyptic, for example. In this way Pauline theology could be public and exoteric, unlike the speculations of the opponents, preserving an "in but not of" the world orientation.

The Spirit has a role, in both prophetic utterance—good and evil spirits (1 Tim 4:1)—and the guidance of authoritative writers (2 Tim 3:15–16). Paul's sense of the Spirit as God's power at work remains, if somewhat altered. Contrast this with Polycarp, for whom the Spirit has almost no role. If the PE are in danger of locking up the Spirit in the structures of an institution, they ably continue Paul's refusal to classify spiritual gifts on the grounds of their apparent extraordinariness.

16. The Patristic theologian Frances Young's *Theology of the Pastoral Letters* is an intelligent and accessible survey.

Those reading the PE for the first or the thirty-first time will be struck by the emphasis upon "sound teaching," healthy doctrine, reinforced by the then popular use of medical analogies. For proponents of pluralism and diversity, this emphasis is likely to seem unhealthy. The principle that healthy nourishment and appropriate discipline produce healthy bodies is, to coin a word, sound. That is the baby; the Pastor's specifics are bath water. That cliché only opens the discussion.

The ecclesiology of the PE attest to distance from Paul. For the Pastor the church is the household of God. "Mystical" language like "Body of Christ" with its speculative development in Colossians and Ephesians is avoided. The household language does not mean that communities are confined to house churches, but rather the opposite. The Pastor does not wish to lose sight of the Christian community as a family. His concept of a family model comes, as urged earlier, from the conservative world of Greco-Roman society.

Size is indicated by the need for various orders, the titles of which, and some functions, remain in use. See the cameo essay on "Church Offices." Especially noteworthy is the existence of an order for unmarried women, "widows," supported by the community.

7. Date

The PE utilize Luke and Acts, issued c. 115.[17] They are in close proximity to Polycarp to the Philippians. Since Polycarp wrote around the time of Ignatius' martyrdom, c. 135, he cannot be dated much earlier than that. See the Introduction to his letter to the Philippians, below. The PE are therefore to be dated c. 125.

8. Reception and Influence

The Pastorals make no clear impression on other texts until Irenaeus, c. 180, who uses them as the benchmark of apostolic orthodoxy. They have never been off the charts since. The Paul of the Pastorals became the standard portrait of Paul, overshadowing if not obliterating, rival constructions. All movements arising in the Renaissance and Reformation looked to the PE for support. Lutheran and Calvinist stress upon justification by faith alone eventually created a bit of distance, leading to critical doubt in the eighteenth century. At that time a challenge to apostolic authorship was

17. As argued by Pervo, *Dating Acts*. This proposal, while gaining adherents, is later than the general consensus.

essentially a challenge to canonicity. This is no longer the case. Many of the objections to Pauline authorship made c. 1775–1850 remain valid. The PE are the most generally acknowledged post-Pauline texts in the NT. In the twentieth century the pastoral Paul had to make some way for revivals of apocalyptic apostles, including proponents of liberation theology, and for renewed interest in a more Gnostic Paul, frank admiration for Marcion, and efforts to overturn justification as the center of Pauline theology.

TITUS

Epistolary Opening

1 Παῦλος δοῦλος θεοῦ, ἀπόστολος δὲ Ἰησοῦ Χριστοῦ κατὰ πίστιν
ἐκλεκτῶν θεοῦ καὶ ἐπίγνωσιν ἀληθείας τῆς κατ’ εὐσέβειαν [2]ἐπ’
ἐλπίδι ζωῆς αἰωνίου, ἣν ἐπηγγείλατο ὁ ἀψευδὴς θεὸς πρὸ χρόνων
αἰωνίων, [3]ἐφανέρωσεν δὲ καιροῖς ἰδίοις τὸν λόγον αὐτοῦ ἐν
κηρύγματι, ὃ ἐπιστεύθην ἐγὼ κατ’ ἐπιταγὴν τοῦ σωτῆρος ἡμῶν θεοῦ,
[4]Τίτῳ γνησίῳ τέκνῳ κατὰ κοινὴν πίστιν, χάρις καὶ εἰρήνη ἀπὸ
θεοῦ πατρὸς καὶ Χριστοῦ Ἰησοῦ τοῦ σωτῆρος ἡμῶν.

Qualifications for Leaders

Presbyters [5]Τούτου χάριν ἀπέλιπόν σε ἐν Κρήτῃ, ἵνα τὰ λείποντα
ἐπιδιορθώσῃ καὶ καταστήσῃς κατὰ πόλιν πρεσβυτέρους, ὡς ἐγώ σοι
διεταξάμην, [6]εἴ τίς ἐστιν ἀνέγκλητος, μιᾶς γυναικὸς ἀνήρ, τέκνα
ἔχων πιστά, μὴ ἐν κατηγορίᾳ ἀσωτίας ἢ ἀνυπότακτα.

Bishops [7]δεῖ γὰρ τὸν ἐπίσκοπον ἀνέγκλητον εἶναι ὡς θεοῦ οἰκονόμον,
μὴ αὐθάδη, μὴ ὀργίλον, μὴ πάροινον, μὴ πλήκτην, μὴ αἰσχροκερδῆ,
[8]ἀλλὰ φιλόξενον φιλάγαθον σώφρονα δίκαιον ὅσιον ἐγκρατῆ,
[9]ἀντεχόμενον τοῦ κατὰ τὴν διδαχὴν πιστοῦ λόγου, ἵνα δυνατὸς ᾖ καὶ
παρακαλεῖν ἐν τῇ διδασκαλίᾳ τῇ ὑγιαινούσῃ καὶ τοὺς ἀντιλέγοντας

1:4 “Compassion” is added to the greeting by a number of witnesses to achieve conformity with 1 Tim 1:2 and 2 Tim 1:2.

1:9 In place of *so that . . . pastoral teaching*, codex Alexandrinus, a whole fifth-century Bible, reads “so that he can comfort those in every sort of stress.”

At the close the Greek-Latin-Arabic ms 460 (thirteenth century) appends: “Do not ordain [as priests] those twice married or make them deacons, or let them take re-married wives. Let not such people approach the altar to serve God. As God’s servant reproach secular leaders who judge unfairly or are robbers or liars or lack compassion.” The editor updates Titus in terms of contemporary canon law. The addition also reflects a situation in which Christian clergy could criticize public officials.

- **1:1–4** This, the most elaborate opening of the three PE, is suitable for the beginning of the collection. Rom 1:1–5 may be its model. Titus, alone among the PE, has no Thanksgiving passage. See “The Pauline Letter,” p. 5.
- **1:3** Note a “theology of the word/message.”
- **1:4** *Valid*, or “genuine” in the sense of legitimate over against, by implication, false followers.
- **1:5–9** The qualifications are simpler than those in 1 Timothy 3. On an historical model—the PE deal with actual situations not only in Ephesus, but also in Crete—the latter community was younger and smaller. A literary model would posit progression from simpler to more complex.
- **1:6–11** See “Catalogues of Virtues and Vices,” p. 19. The positive qualities listed here are those expected of any good citizen in a civic organization. Christians are conventional rather than disruptive of the social order.

Epistolary Opening

1 Paul, slave of God and agent for Jesus Christ for the belief of God's chosen and the genuine knowledge crafted by piety [2]and grounded in hope of unbounded existence, which the utterly reliable God pledged from time immemorial. [3]He has revealed at the appropriate moment his message in the proclamation entrusted to me per the directive of our deliverer God.

[4]To Titus, valid child in the conviction we share, favor and well-being from our fatherly God and the Anointed Jesus, our deliverer.

Qualifications for Leaders

Presbyters

[5]I left you in Crete to straighten up unfinished business and install *presbyters* in every city, as I directed. [6]They should be irreproachable, not remarried, with believing children, unlikely to be accused of raucous behavior or insubordination.

Bishops

[7]Now a *bishop*, as God's manager, is required to be irreproachable, free from insolence, irritability, excessive drinking, violence, or greed. [8]He must rather be hospitable, zealous for the good, judicious, fair, devout, and self-disciplined, [9]maintaining a firm grasp of the trustworthy message we have been taught, so that he can both engage in wholesome pastoral teaching and also refute opponents,

---

- **1:6** *Re-married*. The restriction applies definitely to those divorced and, less likely, to widowers.
- **1:7** *Manager*. Managers have responsibility but not authority. Because many ancient estate managers were formally slaves, the term was apt for Christian leaders, slaves of God: 1 Cor 4:1; Luke 12:42–48; 16:1–8; 1 Pet 4:10.
- **1:8** Beyond its general merits, hospitality was fundamental to the early (and subsequent) Christian mission.

Catalogues of Vices and Virtues

"Catalogues of Vices and Virtues," such as Gal 5:19–21; 22–23, are a common feature of moral exhortation literature. These lists are more general than particular in application. One should not conclude, on the basis of Gal 5:20, for example, that sorcery was a serious problem for the young Christian communities there. The catalogues reflect aspirations and are in that sense exhortations. The Pastor has transformed the category by applying the lists of virtues to prospective leaders while attributing the vices to theological rivals. They have become means for enforcing specific boundaries. Otherwise stated, the catalogues have been integrated into the form of a Church Order, guidelines for the Household of God.

False Teachers

ἐλέγχειν. 10Εἰσὶν γὰρ πολλοὶ [καὶ] ἀνυπότακτοι, ματαιολόγοι καὶ
φρεναπάται, μάλιστα οἱ ἐκ τῆς περιτομῆς, 11οὓς δεῖ ἐπιστομίζειν,
οἵτινες ὅλους οἴκους ἀνατρέπουσιν διδάσκοντες ἃ μὴ δεῖ αἰσχροῦ
κέρδους χάριν. 12εἶπέν τις ἐξ αὐτῶν ἴδιος αὐτῶν προφήτης·

Κρῆτες ἀεὶ ψεῦσται, κακὰ θηρία, γαστέρες ἀργαί.

13ἡ μαρτυρία αὕτη ἐστὶν ἀληθής. δι᾽ ἣν αἰτίαν ἔλεγχε αὐτοὺς
ἀποτόμως, ἵνα ὑγιαίνωσιν ἐν τῇ πίστει, 14μὴ προσέχοντες Ἰουδαϊκοῖς
μύθοις καὶ ἐντολαῖς ἀνθρώπων ἀποστρεφομένων τὴν ἀλήθειαν.
15πάντα καθαρὰ τοῖς καθαροῖς· τοῖς δὲ μεμιαμμένοις καὶ ἀπίστοις
οὐδὲν καθαρόν, ἀλλὰ μεμίανται αὐτῶν καὶ ὁ νοῦς καὶ ἡ συνείδησις.
16θεὸν ὁμολογοῦσιν εἰδέναι, τοῖς δὲ ἔργοις ἀρνοῦνται, βδελυκτοὶ
ὄντες καὶ ἀπειθεῖς καὶ πρὸς πᾶν ἔργον ἀγαθὸν ἀδόκιμοι.

Rules for Household Members

2 Σὺ δὲ λάλει ἃ πρέπει τῇ ὑγιαινούσῃ διδασκαλίᾳ.

Older Men

2Πρεσβύτας νηφαλίους εἶναι, σεμνούς, σώφρονας, ὑγιαίνοντας
τῇ πίστει, τῇ ἀγάπῃ, τῇ ὑπομονῇ·

Women

3Πρεσβύτιδας ὡσαύτως ἐν καταστήματι ἱεροπρεπεῖς, μὴ
διαβόλους μὴ οἴνῳ πολλῷ δεδουλωμένας, καλοδιδασκάλους, 4ἵνα
σωφρονίζωσιν τὰς νέας φιλάνδρους εἶναι, φιλοτέκνους 5σώφρονας
ἁγνὰς οἰκουργοὺς ἀγαθάς, ὑποτασσομένας τοῖς ἰδίοις ἀνδράσιν, ἵνα
μὴ ὁ λόγος τοῦ θεοῦ βλασφημῆται

1:11 After this ms 460 adds, "Stop, reprove, and correct children who hurl abuse or strike their parents, as a father would his own children." This addition views the priest as father of the entire community.
2:5 A variant for *homemakers* is the more common "stay at homes." The words are similar (*oikouros/oikourgos*). Rare words are susceptible of replacement by more familiar terms.

- **1:10–16** Description of rival teachers begins with standard philosophical polemic. The driving (false) assumption is that doctrinal deviance and moral depravity go together. The Pastor's view that suppression of doctrinal discussion is the solution reveals a substantial departure from Paul. The ethnic slur adds local color. (On the quote in v. 12, attributed to Epimenides, see Rothschild, 8–24 and throughout.) Acts 17:28 may have provided inspiration, as the citation, the paradoxical character of which the Pastor overlooks, functions exactly like a scriptural proof text.

  As with church structure, simplicity prevails. The opposition appears to be Torah observant. Eschatological threat (cf. 1 Tim 4:1) is absent. Purity laws/ascetic dietary regulations are simply rejected. Contrast Romans 14. Readers do not yet suspect that "tales" may refer to other than biblical narrative. Cf. 1 Tim 4:3.
- **2:1–15** After denouncing unsound teaching, the Pastor expounds what he deems wholesome. The chapter is marked by an inclusion, repetition of the

[10]for they are numerous, insubordinate, given to stupid, mislead- **False Teachers**
ing yacking, especially those who are Jewish. [11]These teachers, who,
driven by the pursuit of shameful gain, are disturbing entire households and must be squelched. [12]As one of their very own, a prophet,
noted:

"Ah, Cretans: Dishonest, wicked, gluttonous, indolent creatures."

[13]That Cretan was telling the truth. Therefore rebuke them re-
lentlessly, so that they might develop a healthy faith [14]and abandon
Jewish tales and rules devised by people who reject the truth. [15]For
the pure everything is pure; for the defiled and unbelieving nothing
is pure. In fact, both their minds and their consciences are defiled.
[16]They claim that they know God, a contention invalidated by their
actions, since they are abominable, insubordinate, and unfit for
anything worthwhile.

Rules for Household Members

2 For your part, proclaim what conforms to wholesome teaching.
[2]It is seemly that older men be sober, solemn and self-controlled, **Older Men**
sound in belief, concern, and endurance.

[3]Likewise older women should have a demeanor appropriate **Women**
for the devout, avoiding slanderous gossip and dependence upon
alcohol. They should teach what is good. [4]Their mission in to in-
still in young women the good sense to cherish their husbands and
children, [5]to be modest, pure, excellent homemakers, and subordinate to their husbands, so that God's message may not fall into
disrepute.

---

same words at beginning and end. Such devices served ancients as do punctuation and format for us. The content covers much the same ground as the Household Codes in Col 3:18–4:1; Eph 5:22–6:9; 1 Pet 2:18–3:7, but with major differences. Those Codes deal with the rights and duties of three pairs: husbands/wives, parents/children, and owners/slaves. The Pastor adds age categories and says nothing of the obligations of husbands and owners. Contrast with Ephesians, in particular, reveals the absence of effort to "Christianize" the Codes. In vv. 4, 5, 8, and 10 purpose clauses show the goals of these styles. Formally, this is a catalogue of duties. Everyone will do well to avoid the vices deprecated. They are similar to the behavior of the rivals described in 1:10–16.

- **2:3** *Alcohol.* The drunken, gossipy old woman was an ancient stereotype. Until the mid-twentieth century, abuse of alcohol was considered a moral problem, lack of self-control. Alcohol was, to be sure, almost the only analgesic for the pains of aging, let alone those generated by untreated medical and dental problems.
- **2:5** *Modest.* The same word is rendered self-control in v. 6, reflecting different sides of the honor/shame structure. Women avoid shame; men pursue honor, for example, by shaming opponents, v. 8.

Younger Men

6 Τοὺς νεωτέρους ὡσαύτως παρακάλει σωφρονεῖν

Leader as Example

7 περὶ πάντα, σεαυτὸν παρεχόμενος τύπον καλῶν ἔργων, ἐν τῇ
διδασκαλίᾳ ἀφθορίαν, σεμνότητα, 8 λόγον ὑγιῆ ἀκατάγνωστον, ἵνα ὁ
ἐξ ἐναντίας ἐντραπῇ μηδὲν ἔχων λέγειν περὶ ἡμῶν φαῦλον.

Slaves

9 Δούλους ἰδίοις δεσπόταις ὑποτάσσεσθαι ἐν πᾶσιν, εὐαρέστους
εἶναι, μὴ ἀντιλέγοντας, 10 μὴ νοσφιζομένους, ἀλλὰ πᾶσαν πίστιν
ἐνδεικνυμένους ἀγαθήν, ἵνα τὴν διδασκαλίαν τὴν τοῦ σωτῆρος
ἡμῶν θεοῦ κοσμῶσιν ἐν πᾶσιν.

Moral Exhortation

11 Ἐπεφάνη γὰρ ἡ χάρις τοῦ θεοῦ σωτήριος πᾶσιν ἀνθρώποις
12 παιδεύουσα ἡμᾶς, ἵνα ἀρνησάμενοι τὴν ἀσέβειαν καὶ τὰς κοσμικὰς
ἐπιθυμίας σωφρόνως καὶ δικαίως καὶ εὐσεβῶς ζήσωμεν ἐν τῷ νῦν
αἰῶνι, 13 προσδεχόμενοι τὴν μακαρίαν ἐλπίδα καὶ ἐπιφάνειαν τῆς
δόξης τοῦ μεγάλου θεοῦ καὶ σωτῆρος ἡμῶν Ἰησοῦ Χριστοῦ, 14 ὃς
ἔδωκεν ἑαυτὸν ὑπὲρ ἡμῶν, ἵνα λυτρώσηται ἡμᾶς ἀπὸ πάσης ἀνομίας
καὶ καθαρίσῃ ἑαυτῷ λαὸν περιούσιον, ζηλωτὴν καλῶν ἔργων.
15 Ταῦτα λάλει καὶ παρακάλει καὶ ἔλεγχε μετὰ πάσης ἐπιταγῆς· μηδείς
σου περιφρονείτω

3 1 Ὑπομίμνησκε αὐτοὺς

ἀρχαῖς ἐξουσίαις ὑποτάσσεσθαι, πειθαρχεῖν,
πρὸς πᾶν ἔργον ἀγαθὸν ἑτοίμους εἶναι,
2 μηδένα βλασφημεῖν,
ἀμάχους εἶναι,
ἐπιεικεῖς, πᾶσαν ἐνδεικνυμένους πραΰτητα πρὸς πάντας
ἀνθρώπους.

2:8 Several variants for *irreproachable* are similar in form: "free of envy," "sincere," and, a spelling error, "indifferent."
3:2 The important fourth-century Bible Sinaiticus reads, instead of *showing everyone respect*, "to demonstrate zeal."

- **2:9–10** Stereotypes about ancient slaves included pilfering and "playing dumb" to evade work. We are inclined to say "good for them." This is not the high point of early Christian ethics.
- **2:11–14** Power to accomplish the foregoing virtues comes at the end. *Generosity* (grace), here given the status of an epiphany, is educative.
- **2:13** The contrast is not quite "now vs. not yet," nor do we behave ourselves in order to be saved. Present and future are linked, if not clearly. Christ is acquiring a larger soteriological role while still clearly subordinate to God. Theology is in transition.

[6]In the same way encourage the younger men to exhibit self-control. **Younger Men**

[7]Set out to be a model for every kind of good deed, exhibit- **Leader as Example**
ing integrity in teaching, gravity, [8]and irreproachably wholesome
preaching, so that an opponent will look ridiculous if he tries to say something bad about us.

[9]As for slaves: they are to exhibit full and cheerful subordination **Slaves**
to their masters, with no back talk or [10]thievery, rather displaying
perfectly excellent fidelity, serving as ornaments of our deliverer God in every respect.

Moral Exhortation

[11]For God's liberating generosity for all people has arrived. [12]This
trains us to lead moderate, just and pious lives in this era by repud-
ing impiety and ungodly passions, [13]as we look forward to the hoped
for happy arrival of our majestic great God and of our liberator Jesus
Christ. [14]Christ gave himself for us to rescue us from all lawless deeds
and refine a special people of his very own, eager for good deeds.
[15]These are what you should say. Urge and correct authoritatively.
Don't let anyone treat you as an inferior.

3 Some things to have them keep in mind:

> to submit to and obey officials and authority figures;
> to remain alert for every opportunity to do good;
> [2]to slander no one;
> to be peaceable;
> to be mild, showing everyone full respect.

Great was an epithet of monarchs and "Eastern" gods in particular, but not exclusively. Cf. Acts 19:28. It especially endures in Islam. The language used to describe God and Christ has its roots in the ruler cult, which presented a familiar theology and vocabulary for identifying and praising the presence of the divine in current history.

- **2:14** Christ's redemptive self-offering (cf. Gal 1:4) grounds the final purpose clause, rescue from evil and refinement. The latter (lit. "cleanse") may refer to baptism. The Pastor knows that Christ came not only to save sinners (1 Tim 1:15).
- **3:1–2, 8** To his credit, the Pastor maintains Paul's view that following Christ does not remove believers from the world but frees them for service to others, including non-believers. Furthermore, the directives have Christian motives.
- **3:1** Obedience to rulers reflects the desire for public acceptance. In the AcPaul 4 Thecla battles a priest of the emperor cult, threatening the royal image (a highly unpatriotic act altered in the Greek mss).

[3]Ἦμεν γάρ ποτε καὶ ἡμεῖς ἀνόητοι, ἀπειθεῖς, πλανώμενοι,
δουλεύοντες ἐπιθυμίαις καὶ ἡδοναῖς ποικίλαις, ἐν κακίᾳ καὶ φθόνῳ
διάγοντες, στυγητοί, μισοῦντες ἀλλήλους.
[4]ὅτε δὲ ἡ χρηστότης καὶ ἡ φιλανθρωπία ἐπεφάνη τοῦ σωτῆρος
ἡμῶν θεοῦ,

[5]οὐκ ἐξ ἔργων τῶν ἐν δικαιοσύνῃ
ἃ ἐποιήσαμεν ἡμεῖς
ἀλλὰ κατὰ τὸ αὐτοῦ ἔλεος
ἔσωσεν ἡμᾶς διὰ λουτροῦ παλιγγενεσίας
καὶ ἀνακαινώσεως πνεύματος ἁγίου, [6]οὗ ἐξέχεεν ἐφ' ἡμᾶς
πλουσίως
διὰ Ἰησοῦ Χριστοῦ τοῦ σωτῆρος ἡμῶν,

[7]ἵνα δικαιωθέντες τῇ ἐκείνου χάριτι κληρονόμοι γενηθῶμεν κατ'
ἐλπίδα ζωῆς αἰωνίου.
[8]Πιστὸς ὁ λόγος·
καὶ περὶ τούτων βούλομαί σε διαβεβαιοῦσθαι, ἵνα φροντίζωσιν
καλῶν ἔργων προΐστασθαι οἱ πεπιστευκότες θεῷ· ταῦτά ἐστιν καλὰ
καὶ ὠφέλιμα τοῖς ἀνθρώποις.

Rival Beliefs

[9]μωρὰς δὲ ζητήσεις καὶ γενεαλογίας καὶ ἔρεις καὶ μάχας νομικὰς
περιΐστασο· εἰσὶν γὰρ ἀνωφελεῖς καὶ μάταιοι.
[10]αἱρετικὸν ἄνθρωπον μετὰ μίαν καὶ δευτέραν νουθεσίαν
παραιτοῦ, [11]εἰδὼς ὅτι ἐξέστραπται ὁ τοιοῦτος καὶ ἁμαρτάνει ὢν
αὐτοκατάκριτος.
[12]Ὅταν πέμψω Ἀρτεμᾶν πρὸς σὲ ἢ Τύχικον, σπούδασον ἐλθεῖν
πρός με εἰς Νικόπολιν, ἐκεῖ γὰρ κέκρικα παραχειμάσαι. [13]Ζηνᾶν τὸν

- **3:4–7** This quasi-hymnic passage represents a common theme of early Christian proclamation, contrasting past error and misery to present joy and righteous behavior. Paul also stresses the result of faith, but the Pastor clearly states the necessity of good works.
- **3:4** *Benevolent generosity*. Only here is the term *philanthrōpia* used of God in the NT.
- **3:5** *New birth*. This is the clearest statement of baptismal regeneration in the NT.
- **3:6** *Pour*. This apt metaphor may be due to Acts 2:17–33.
- **3:9** The author's refusal to engage in debate may sound high-minded, but it raises the suspicion that the opponents were likely to win arguments. Subjects to be avoided can be understood in terms of the Torah—descent from Abraham and the place of Law—but they could also apply to speculation about creation and/or symbolic interpretations of cultic regulations.
- **3:10** *Dissenters*. Literally, "factious persons." Factionalism was widely disparaged. Minority and/or excluded groups rarely raised this complaint. The

[3]For we were once foolish, impudent, fooled, addicted to various desires and pleasures, devoting our days to wickedness and envy, hateful and hated. [4]But when the benevolent generosity of our liberating God arrived, freedom followed,

> [5]Not because we did the right things,
> but because of compassion,
> through the bath of new birth
> and new life [6]bestowed by the holy spirit, abundantly poured
> upon us
> through Jesus Christ our liberator,

[7]so that, made acceptable to God through his gift, we might hope to inherit unbounded existence.

[8]That's the gospel truth.

In this regard I direct you to insist that those who have come to trust in God attend seriously to accomplishing good deeds, which are not only good but also profitable for others.

Rival Beliefs

[9]On the other hand, avoid stupid controversies and efforts to trace things to their origins, as well as quarrels and legal disputes, as they are unprofitable wastes of time.

[10]Get rid of dissenters after two admonitions; [11]you know such people are misled and that their continued erring amounts to self-refutation.

[12]As soon as I can send you either Artemas or Tychicus meet me promptly at Nicopolis, where I have decided to winter.

---

ultimate objects are pastoral, unity and correction of the wayward, but the shadow of v. 9 hangs over this command.

- **3:12–14** Paul's letters usually include travel plans, a highlight of which is the "apostolic parousia," his impending visit, e.g. Rom 15:14–33. Here the model is inverted: disciple is to visit apostle.
- **3:12** The mask evanesces. After giving Titus detailed instructions for the organization of communities on Crete, "Paul" tells him to drop everything and hasten to Nicopolis. This is scarcely mitigated by the possibility of sending in Artemas or Tychicus to deputize for Titus.
- **3:12** *Artemas.* Other than edifying legendary guesses, nothing is known about this person.

  Tychicus. An Asian who accompanied Paul and the collection to Jerusalem (cf. Acts 20:4). He is identified as the carrier of (the Deuteropauline) Colossians (4:7–8) and Ephesians (6:21–22).

  Nicopolis was in Epirus (modern Albania), evidently a prospective mission field.

νομικὸν καὶ Ἀπολλῶν σπουδαίως πρόπεμψον, ἵνα μηδὲν αὐτοῖς
λείπῃ. [14]μανθανέτωσαν δὲ καὶ οἱ ἡμέτεροι καλῶν ἔργων προΐστασθαι
εἰς τὰς ἀναγκαίας χρείας, ἵνα μὴ ὦσιν ἄκαρποι.

Epistolary Close

[15]Ἀσπάζονταί σε οἱ μετ᾽ ἐμοῦ πάντες. ἄσπασαι τοὺς φιλοῦντας ἡμᾶς ἐν πίστει.

Ἡ χάρις μετὰ πάντων ὑμῶν.

3:15 The closing "grace," addressed to a plural audience, was altered to "and with your [sing.] spirit," to conform to the ostensible addressee.

Various "notes" on the epistle, including data on where it was written, who carried it, and Titus' résumé were added to later mss.

• **3:13** *Zenas the lawyer.* He would presumably have been a legal expert who could assist Paul in his case. The Acts of Titus 1 credits him as the author of that work.

[13]Carefully arrange full travel expenses for Zenas the lawyer and
for Apollos.[14]Make sure that our people learn to take up good em-
ployment and be able to meet pressing obligations rather than be
unproductive.

Epistolary Close

[15]Everyone here sends their greetings. Greet the believers who
cherish us.

God's favor be with all of you.

- **3:13** *Apollos.* As can be seen from the confused account in Acts 18–19 and 1 Corinthians, Apollos was an independent missionary. By this brief reference the Pastor indicates his complete subordination to the apostle.
- **3:15** The plural *all of you* envisions a broader audience than Titus.

1 TIMOTHY

Epistolary Opening

1 Παῦλος

ἀπόστολος Χριστοῦ Ἰησοῦ
κατ᾽ ἐπιταγὴν θεοῦ σωτῆρος ἡμῶν
καὶ Χριστοῦ Ἰησοῦ τῆς ἐλπίδος ἡμῶν
[2]Τιμοθέῳ γνησίῳ τέκνῳ ἐν πίστει,
χάρις ἔλεος εἰρήνη ἀπὸ θεοῦ πατρὸς καὶ Χριστοῦ Ἰησοῦ τοῦ
κυρίου ἡμῶν.

The Place of Law

[3]Καθὼς παρεκάλεσά σε προσμεῖναι ἐν Ἐφέσῳ πορευόμενος εἰς
Μακεδονίαν, ἵνα παραγγείλῃς τισὶν μὴ ἑτεροδιδασκαλεῖν [4]μηδὲ
προσέχειν μύθοις καὶ γενεαλογίαις ἀπεράντοις, αἵτινες ἐκζητήσεις
παρέχουσιν μᾶλλον ἢ οἰκονομίαν θεοῦ τὴν ἐν πίστει.

[5]τὸ δὲ τέλος τῆς παραγγελίας ἐστὶν ἀγάπη ἐκ καθαρᾶς καρδίας
καὶ συνειδήσεως ἀγαθῆς καὶ πίστεως ἀνυποκρίτου, [6]ὧν τινες
ἀστοχήσαντες ἐξετράπησαν εἰς ματαιολογίαν [7]θέλοντες εἶναι
νομοδιδάσκαλοι, μὴ νοοῦντες μήτε ἃ λέγουσιν μήτε περὶ τίνων
διαβεβαιοῦνται. [8]Οἴδαμεν δὲ ὅτι καλὸς ὁ νόμος, ἐάν τις αὐτῷ
νομίμως χρῆται, [9]εἰδὼς τοῦτο, ὅτι δικαίῳ νόμος οὐ κεῖται, ἀνόμοις δὲ
καὶ ἀνυποτάκτοις, ἀσεβέσι καὶ ἁμαρτωλοῖς, ἀνοσίοις καὶ βεβήλοις,

---

1:1 For *directive* a single ms (Sinaiticus, a fourth-century entire Bible) substitutes "promise," a more Pauline term although not appropriate here.
1:4 For *the way God has done things* (*oikonomia*) a D-Text variant is the more common "edification" (*oikodomē*).

- **1:1–2** The opening of this letter, like the closing, is quite succinct, qualities not optimal for the first text in a collection.
- **1:1** *Agent*. Paul is the only apostle in the PE.
- **1:1** *Directive* instead of the typically Pauline "promise." This phrase is common for indicating fulfillment of religious vows.
- **1:1** The PE prefer the order *the Anointed Jesus*.
- **1:2** Paul calls converts "children" in the spiritual sense. For Timothy see 1 Cor 4:17. In the PE the word acquires a paternalistic aura.
- **1:2** *Fatherly God*, lit. "God the father." "Creator" lacks the sense of warmth and personality. "Loving Parent" is an alternative, but the PE are unrelentingly patriarchal.
- **1:3** Movement by Paul from Ephesus to Macedonia is described in the 2 Corinthian correspondence (2:12–13; 7:5–6). Neither that nor Acts can be fit into this picture. According to Acts 20:17–38, presbyters were in charge of the community.

Epistolary Opening

1 Paul,

An agent for the Anointed Jesus
in pursuance of the directive of God our liberator
and the Anointed Jesus our hope.
2To Timothy, cherished child in the conviction we share
favor, compassion, and wellbeing
from our fatherly God and the Anointed Jesus, our master.

The Place of Law

3Do not disregard what I told you when I was leaving for
Macedonia: Stay in Ephesus and enjoin certain people from spread-
ing a deviant message 4or focusing upon improbable tales or endless
attempts to trace matters back to origins, which nurture speculation
rather than faithful reflection upon the way God has done things.
5This precept seeks to result in affection that arises from a pure
heart, a sound conscience, and sincere trust. 6Certain individuals
have not stuck to these goals and have drifted into useless yakking.
7They would like to promulgate laws, but they have no idea what
they are saying or the matters about which they propound asser-
tions. 8To be sure, we understand that the law is good, when properly applied, 9that is, law is not set up for law-abiding people but for
law-breakers and the insubordinate, for the impious, wrong-doing,

---

- **1:3–20** The structure moves from false teaching (3–11), to thanksgiving with personal example (12–17), then back to false teaching (18–20).
- **1:3–11** No consensus about the views of the Pastor's opponents has emerged. A strong Jewish element is apparent, but its focus is not clear. "Improbable tales or endless attempts to trace matters back to origins" might indicate indulgence in speculation about Genesis 1–3. Opposing these views is a general appeal to salvation history (v. 4). Other issues will emerge. For the Pastor law refers to ethical commandments, not to a way of life, nor, as Paul argued, a means for revealing sin.
- **1:5** *Conscience* in Paul often means consciousness; for the Pastor it is an instrument for making proper decisions. For Paul conscience is a tool of freedom; for the Pastor conscience limits freedom.
- **1:8** *We understand* is a pastoral expression reminding the audience of the material at their disposal.
- **1:9** *Law abiding*, lit. "just," a clearly non-Pauline use of term.
- **1:9–10** This Catalogue of Vices (see p. 19) is rooted in the Decalogue. Law deals with major ethical categories.
- **1:9** In place of honoring parents (e.g. Exod 20:12), one is not to murder them. The bar is not getting higher.

πατρολῴαις καὶ μητρολῴαις, ἀνδροφόνοις [10]πόρνοις ἀρσενοκοίταις
ἀνδραποδισταῖς ψεύσταις ἐπιόρκοις, καὶ εἴ τι ἕτερον τῇ ὑγιαινούσῃ
διδασκαλίᾳ ἀντίκειται [11]κατὰ τὸ εὐαγγέλιον τῆς δόξης τοῦ μακαρίου
θεοῦ, ὃ ἐπιστεύθην ἐγώ.

Paul's Example

[12]Χάριν ἔχω τῷ ἐνδυναμώσαντί με Χριστῷ Ἰησοῦ τῷ κυρίῳ ἡμῶν,
ὅτι πιστόν με ἡγήσατο θέμενος εἰς διακονίαν [13]τὸ πρότερον ὄντα
βλάσφημον καὶ διώκτην καὶ ὑβριστήν, ἀλλὰ ἠλεήθην, ὅτι ἀγνοῶν
ἐποίησα ἐν ἀπιστίᾳ· [14]ὑπερεπλεόνασεν δὲ ἡ χάρις τοῦ κυρίου ἡμῶν

• **1:10** The injunction against adultery is expanded by reference to male-male sexual acts. The perspective is androcentric. "Homosexuality" is an errone-

The Structure of 1 Timothy

Linda Maloney* proposes that 1 Timothy exhibits a concentric or chiastic pattern. Chiasmus (A B B A) is an aesthetic device with various implications.

Glory to you	A
Beholding the Depths	B
In the High Vault of Heaven	B
Glory to You	A

This figure of speech aids memory. Chiasmus thrusts emphasis toward the center (whence "concentric"). This is apparent in the above example from the Song of the Three Young Men; it is even more apparent when the number of members is odd: A B C B A. There is a deeper sense, perceptible in poems and hymns that have a framing stanza: you can't go home again, for what you read the first time has changed in meaning when encountered again.

Maloney proposes:

1:1–20	A
2:1–3:13	B
4	C (repetition of A themes)
5:1–6:2c	B
6:2d–21	A

An advantage of this scheme is that it shows how distant 1 Timothy is from the typical Pauline letter structure, which may have connections between opening and closing but not this kind of internal cohesion.

*"The Pastoral Epistles," 366–68

unholy and utterly profane: murderers of their father or mother,
killers, [10]the sexually immoral, males who sleep with males, human
traffickers, liars, perjurers, and whatever else conflicts with wholesome instruction, [11]that is, the glorious message of the beneficent
God which has been entrusted to me.

Paul's Example

[12]I am grateful to our master, the Anointed Jesus, who has em-
powered me because he deemed me trustworthy by appointing me
to service[13]—me, a former slanderer, persecutor, and insolent oaf—
but I was treated with compassion, because I did what I did in ignorant unbelief. [14]Our master's generosity inundated me with the trust

---

ous understanding, for behavior, not orientation, is in view, and males, at least elite ones, had a range of sexual partners.

On sound or wholesome teaching, see "Sound Teaching," below.

- **1:11** *Glorious message* ("gospel") applies to the entire proclamation, with special emphasis upon its moral dimension. This is decidedly non-Pauline.
- **1:12–17** Thanksgivings normally precede the body of Pauline letters, e.g. Rom 1:8–12. Paul, however, thanks God, not Christ. Here "Paul" gives thanks for his own conversion. He is portrayed as a gentile sinner. This does not conform to the historical Paul, e.g., Phil 3:4–7. The purpose is to provide a model for gentile converts. Conversion accounts, individual and corporate, typically describe sweeping transformations, from darkness to light, ignorance to truth, sin to righteousness. Greco-Roman biography tended to serve moral rather than historical ends.

Sound Teaching

This medical metaphor, which employs the adjective *hygiēs* (1 time) and the derived verb (8 times; cf. English "hygiene"), is unique to and characteristic of the PE. The metaphor comes from popular philosophical polemic. "I'll give 'em a strong dose of medicine for that" aptly continues its ancient function. Ancient philosophers and theologians evidently digested a lot of medical literature. The imagery embraces the corporate notion of the church as a body, but the focus is reduced to content, doctrine or teaching. This medical imagery is typical of the Pastor because it presumes that Christianity is a rational phenomenon that will respond to rational analysis and treatment. This is quite unlike Paul, of course, and betrays a step—and not a small step—toward the world of the apologists, who sought to give Christianity a rational grounding.

μετὰ πίστεως καὶ ἀγάπης τῆς ἐν Χριστῷ Ἰησοῦ. [15]πιστὸς ὁ λόγος καὶ
πάσης ἀποδοχῆς ἄξιος, ὅτι Χριστὸς Ἰησοῦς ἦλθεν εἰς τὸν κόσμον
ἁμαρτωλοὺς σῶσαι, ὧν πρῶτός εἰμι ἐγώ.
[16]ἀλλὰ διὰ τοῦτο ἠλεήθην, ἵνα ἐν ἐμοὶ πρώτῳ ἐνδείξηται Χριστὸς
Ἰησοῦς τὴν ἅπασαν μακροθυμίαν πρὸς ὑποτύπωσιν τῶν μελλόντων
πιστεύειν ἐπ' αὐτῷ εἰς ζωὴν αἰώνιον. [17]Τῷ δὲ βασιλεῖ τῶν αἰώνων,
ἀφθάρτῳ ἀοράτῳ μόνῳ θεῷ, τιμὴ καὶ δόξα εἰς τοὺς αἰῶνας τῶν
αἰώνων, ἀμήν.

Timothy's Task

[18]Ταύτην τὴν παραγγελίαν παρατίθεμαί σοι, τέκνον Τιμόθεε,
κατὰ τὰς προαγούσας ἐπὶ σὲ προφητείας, ἵνα στρατεύῃ ἐν αὐταῖς τὴν
καλὴν στρατείαν [19]ἔχων πίστιν καὶ ἀγαθὴν συνείδησιν,

Negative Examples

ἥν τινες ἀπωσάμενοι περὶ τὴν πίστιν ἐναυάγησαν, [20]ὧν
ἐστιν Ὑμέναιος καὶ Ἀλέξανδρος, οὓς παρέδωκα τῷ σατανᾷ, ἵνα
παιδευθῶσιν μὴ βλασφημεῖν.

Rules for the Household of God

Prayers for Authorities

2 Παρακαλῶ οὖν πρῶτον πάντων ποιεῖσθαι δεήσεις προσευχὰς
ἐντεύξεις εὐχαριστίας ὑπὲρ πάντων ἀνθρώπων, [2]ὑπὲρ βασιλέων
καὶ πάντων τῶν ἐν ὑπεροχῇ ὄντων, ἵνα ἤρεμον καὶ ἡσύχιον βίον
διάγωμεν ἐν πάσῃ εὐσεβείᾳ καὶ σεμνότητι.

1:17 For *imperishable* some D-Text witnesses read "immortal." Others add it to the list.
2:1 Several D-Text witnesses make the *primary directive* a singular command, "direct."

- **1:15** *Gospel truth* is modern American idiom for "the saying is trustworthy." This is a means for identifying and underlining traditional material. That is aptly illustrated here, for statements about Jesus' coming (Mark 1:38, also common in John, e.g. 1:9; 3:17) are summary reflections upon his ministry.
- **1:15** *Liberate wrongdoers.* Many American evangelicals understand this phrase to mean "Jesus Christ came into the world to punish sinners."
- **1:16** The PE make frequent use of exemplary figures.
- **1:17** The doxology has its background in Hellenistic Judaism, possibly synagogue worship.
- **1:18** *Prophecies.* See Acts 13:1–3, possibly the source. See also 1 Tim 4:14 and 2 Tim 1:6.
- **1:18** *Honorable campaign.* Military imagery (cf. 2 Tim 2:3–4) serves to stress discipline and strenuous labor. Such imagery was quite widely used in antiquity.
- **1:20** Naming opponents is atypical. The practice lends vividness to the PE. They may well be fictitious. Alexander, for example, shares a name with a

and love that reside in the Anointed Jesus. [15]This is gospel truth that deserves unqualified acceptance: the Anointed Jesus came into the world to liberate wrongdoers, of whom I am the foremost example.

[16]I was treated with compassion so that the Anointed Jesus might display me as the foremost example of his utmost patience to those who will trust him as the source of unbounded existence. [17]To the monarch of the ages, the imperishable, invisible, only God, we give honor and glory, for ever and ever, amen.

Timothy's Task

[18]I am transmitting this directive to you, my dear child Timothy, in light of the earlier prophecies about you, so that you, in pursuance of them, might wage the honorable campaign, [19]armed with trust and a sound conscience.

Negative Examples

Some people have rejected the guidance of conscience and made a shipwreck of the faith. [20]These include Hymenaeus and Alexander, whom I have turned over to Satan for discipline against blasphemy.

Rules for the Household of God

Prayers for Authorities

2 My primary directive is that entreaties, petitions, intercessions, and thanksgivings be offered for all people: [2]for monarchs and all of high rank, so that we might lead tranquil and undisrupted lives in all godly dignity.

---

figure in the disturbance at Ephesus generated by silversmiths (Acts 19:23). Alexander the coppersmith in 2 Tim 2:14 is also a metalworker. Hymenaeus is identified as a false teacher in 2 Tim 2:17.

- **1:20** *Turned over*. This is a form of excommunication. Cf. 1 Cor 5:5 and contrast that passage to this. There the community was to act. Here Paul is the sole agent. Note also Acts 5:1–11. The notion that the apostle had magical powers should not be excluded from consideration.
- **2:1–6:2** constitute the body of this letter.
- **2:1–8** are marked by an inclusion.
- **2:1** Universality is a recurrent theme. Believers' prayers, no less than their good deeds, are not confined to the household of God.
- **2:2** Prayers for rulers show that Christians are law-abiding citizens. One might expect the Pastor to proceed down the social hierarchy, but he moves on to a purpose clause. This can be understood as what believers wish from rulers: non-persecution. It also expresses indirectly how the faithful are to behave. The goal (which appears in the reference to "domestic tranquility" in the preamble to the U. S. Constitution) is good if the means of avoiding disruption are not repressive. For another perspective see the Acts of Paul, in which Thecla dashes the imperial image to the ground (4) and Paul confronts the emperor in person (14).

[3]τοῦτο καλὸν καὶ ἀπόδεκτον ἐνώπιον τοῦ σωτῆρος ἡμῶν θεοῦ,
[4]ὃς πάντας ἀνθρώπους θέλει σωθῆναι καὶ εἰς ἐπίγνωσιν ἀληθείας
ἐλθεῖν.

[5]εἷς γὰρ θεός,
εἷς καὶ μεσίτης θεοῦ καὶ ἀνθρώπων,
ἄνθρωπος Χριστὸς Ἰησοῦς,
[6]ὁ δοὺς ἑαυτὸν ἀντίλυτρον ὑπὲρ πάντων,
τὸ μαρτύριον καιροῖς ἰδίοις.

Paul's Mission

[7]εἰς ὃ ἐτέθην ἐγὼ κῆρυξ καὶ ἀπόστολος, ἀλήθειαν λέγω οὐ ψεύδομαι,
διδάσκαλος ἐθνῶν ἐν πίστει καὶ ἀληθείᾳ.
[8]Βούλομαι οὖν προσεύχεσθαι τοὺς ἄνδρας ἐν παντὶ τόπῳ
ἐπαίροντας ὁσίους χεῖρας χωρὶς ὀργῆς καὶ διαλογισμοῦ.

Women

[9]Ὡσαύτως [καὶ] γυναῖκας ἐν καταστολῇ κοσμίῳ μετὰ αἰδοῦς
καὶ σωφροσύνης κοσμεῖν ἑαυτάς, μὴ ἐν πλέγμασιν καὶ χρυσίῳ

2:7 "By Christ" is added to the affirmation of truth telling by many witnesses. The source is Rom 9:1.

- **2:3–4** Prayers for rulers will evidently both please God and promote the universal mission.
- **2:4** *Come to know the truth.* This is equivalent to conversion.
- **2:5–6** Expression of the divine will motivates the Pastor to offer a brief creedal statement. The Jewish declaration of *one God* is not simply anti-polytheistic; it reflects and nurtures the notion of the one people, Israel, God's people. For Christians it retains some of this community-building function, but the theological claim takes first place. To this is added a second: Jesus, whose humanity is stressed. *Mediator* can have several meanings. One is the go-between who conveys essential information. In that capacity Jesus replaces Moses. Another is the agent who helps resolve disputes. Jesus accomplishes that task not through negotiation but by paying the bill through self-offering. Cf. Mark 10:45. For the Pastor that self-offering was not only signing the check. It was testimony, world-shattering witness, that unites Jesus with subsequent martyrs. One may compare and contrast this with the Christology based upon the model of a savior who descends and ascends (Phil 2:6–11; John).
- **2:7** See 2 Tim 1:11.
- **2:9–15** After a verse about men, the Pastor engages in what amounts to a rant against women. Only with difficulty can one maintain that these are instructions relating to worship. It is thus marked as an excursus. Whatever his personal psychological profile, about which we know nothing, the Pastor had a "thing" about women. Two apparent causes are the desire for social respectability and the attraction of women toward the rival teachers. (After reading this passage, contemporary readers are likely to understand that attraction.) These are not offered as mitigations. Perhaps the principal learning for those of today is the truth that movements, religious and other,

3Such prayers are good and acceptable in the view of our liberating God, 4who wishes all people to be freed and come to know the
truth.

> 5There is but one God
> and a single mediator between God and humankind,
> the Anointed Jesus, human himself.
> 6He gave himself as a means of liberation for all,
> as testimony at the right moment.

Paul's Mission

7For this testimony I was appointed proclaimer and agent—this
is the truth; I do not lie—a trustworthy and reliable instructor of
gentiles.
8It is, then, my desire that the men in every locality should pray,
raising holy hands without rancorous dispute.

Women

9As for women, I want them to appear modestly and moderately
dressed, in appropriate outfits without elaborate hairdos, gold jew-

---

come equipped with substantial cultural baggage. This passage should lead all readers to take such challenges quite seriously. They also dispel any notions that everything in the Bible, or any other foundational text, contains nothing but timeless and eternal truth. Most of this material is commonplace. How much it resembles reality beyond the realm of male locker-room bragging is often debatable.

- **2:9–10** Strictures about female attire and coiffures are quite general (and enduring). These are clearly not restricted to worship.
- **2:9** *I want* is a polite imperative.

Piety

One hears that the Greeks had a word for it. One "it" for which they did not have a word was "religion." First, note that ancients did not separate religion from other spheres of life, such as politics. "Separation of church and state" would have made as much sense to the average Roman as the proposal that they use nuclear weapons against their Iranian adversaries. If necessity demands a Greek word for religion, a contender would be *eusebeia.* This term occurs 1 time in Acts, 4 times in 2 Peter, and 10 times in the PE. Its fundamental meaning is reverence toward that to which reverence is due, including the gods and one's parents. A common derivative meaning is suitable expression of that piety through actions.

Eusebeia is a very important word for the Pastor, characteristic of his outlook and orientation toward religiosity. It represents the kind of godliness that we house next door to cleanliness, that is, what respectable people do. In most instances it is rendered here as "piety."

ἢ μαργαρίταις ἢ ἱματισμῷ πολυτελεῖ 10ἀλλ’ ὃ πρέπει γυναιξὶν
ἐπαγγελλομέναις θεοσέβειαν, δι’ ἔργων ἀγαθῶν. 11Γυνὴ ἐν ἡσυχίᾳ
μανθανέτω ἐν πάσῃ ὑποταγῇ· 12διδάσκειν δὲ γυναικὶ οὐκ ἐπιτρέπω
οὐδὲ αὐθεντεῖν ἀνδρός, ἀλλ’ εἶναι ἐν ἡσυχίᾳ. 13δὰμ γὰρ πρῶτος
ἐπλάσθη, εἶτα Εὕα. 14καὶ Ἀδὰμ οὐκ ἠπατήθη, ἡ δὲ γυνὴ ἐξαπατηθεῖσα
ἐν παραβάσει γέγονεν· 15σωθήσεται δὲ διὰ τῆς τεκνογονίας, ἐὰν
μείνωσιν ἐν πίστει καὶ ἀγάπῃ καὶ ἁγιασμῷ μετὰ σωφροσύνης

Church Officers

Bishops

3 Πιστὸς ὁ λόγος. Εἴ τις ἐπισκοπῆς ὀρέγεται, καλοῦ ἔργου ἐπιθυμεῖ.
2δεῖ οὖν τὸν ἐπίσκοπον ἀνεπίλημπτον εἶναι, μιᾶς γυναικὸς ἄνδρα,
νηφάλιον σώφρονα κόσμιον φιλόξενον διδακτικόν, 3μὴ πάροινον
μὴ πλήκτην, ἀλλὰ ἐπιεικῆ ἄμαχον ἀφιλάργυρον, 4τοῦ ἰδίου οἴκου
καλῶς προϊστάμενον, τέκνα ἔχοντα ἐν ὑποταγῇ, μετὰ πάσης

3:1 A number of D-Text witnesses have, instead of the *gospel truth* formula, "as one often hears." The same variant occurs at 1 Tim 1:15, but here it has a good claim to be original. The phrase would go with the following, affirming that the pursuit of office is virtuous.
3:3 After *bully* many later witnesses add "not avaricious," taken from Titus 1:7. This illustrates the tendency of texts to become contaminated by one another.

- **2:11–15** Now the Pastor lets loose. Vv. 11–12 are the source of the interpolation in 1 Cor 14:33b–35. To understand these naked imperatives one may turn to their mirror image in the Acts of Paul, especially 3–4, where Thecla does and says everything that the Pastor abhors (save in the matter of fancy hairdos and frocks, which exercise no appeal for her), and where women elsewhere regularly prophesy in church. Vv. 13–14 are clever, if, as suspected, some women are speculating about Genesis 1–3 (cf. 1 Corinthians 11). The Pastor seeks to administer to them a dose of their own medicine. This betrays awareness of Jewish traditions that postulated the seduction of Eve by the serpent, in addition to the priority of the male in creation as warrant for authority. Keeping his eyes on Gen 3:16—to the woman *God* said, "I will greatly increase your pangs in childbearing; in pain you shall bring forth children, yet your desire shall be for your husband, and he shall rule over you"—the author finds a way out for women: child-bearing. Nothing could be further from Paul (1 Corinthians 7). Prohibition of marriage is a charge made against rival teachers (1 Tim 4:3).
- **3:1–13** present qualifications for the offices of *bishop* and *deacon*. Duties of the former are apparent: preaching, teaching, and pastoral discipline. Diaconal duties are not specified. This may because the actual audience was aware of these duties. *Bishops* are not simply heads of house-based churches, as each has his own household (v. 5). The model assumes a growing community. The implicit model is the manager. Cf. Titus 1:7.
- **3:2–7** The list of qualifications is quite similar to that for presbyters in 1:6–9.

elry, pearls, or expensive clothes—none of that! [10]The best fashion
for women who profess piety is good deeds. [11]Women are to learn
in silence marked by utter submission. [12]I do not permit a woman
to teach or exercise authority over a man. I do permit them to be
silent. [13]Remember that Adam was created with priority; Eve came
second. [14]Additionally, Adam did not take the bait, but the woman
did and thus sinned. [15]Women will, however, be rescued by child-
bearing, provided that they persist in trust, affection, and holiness
marked by modesty.

Church Officers

Bishops

3 A gospel truth: whoever aspires to a supervisory position is
looking for a good calling. [2]Now a *bishop* is required to be irreproachable, not married after divorce, temperate, judicious, respectable,
hospitable, a good teacher, [3]not a heavy drinker, not a bully, kind,
not quarrelsome, not unduly fond of money, [4]excellently direct-
ing his own household, fully controlling his children with dignity.

- **3:2, 12** Since polygamy is not in the picture and remarriage after the death of a spouse is acceptable (1 Tim 5:11), the most likely meaning is that officers who are divorcés are not to marry. It might mean that they may not marry divorced women.
- **3:4–5** See Polycarp 11:2 for a very similar sentiment.

Church Offices in the Pastoral Epistles

The Pastorals refer to *Episkopoi, Presbyteroi, Diakonoi* (evidently both men and women), and an order of widows. These receive support from the community (1 Timothy 5). All three offices still exist: bishops, presbyters, and deacons in communities with the traditional orders of ministry, and with various titles and functions in the several denominations.

The Pastor writes a good deal about the qualifications of these officers, but says relatively little about their function. Functional translations, such as overseer, elder/senior, and servant are therefore misleading. For this reason the translation uses the traditional *bishop, presbyter,* and *deacon* in italics. Although *bishop* occurs only in the singular, *presbyters* can exercise pastoral jurisdiction. They, however, are generally viewed as a body, the *presbyterion* (1 Tim 4:14). The author may acknowledge that some communities are headed by *presbyters*, others by *bishops*. Debate has been long and arduous. The Pastor is aware of the kind of monarchical bishop envisioned by Ignatius of Antioch (d. c. 135), for he presumes that both Timothy and Titus are the single heads of their respective communities.

σεμνότητος. [5](εἰ δέ τις τοῦ ἰδίου οἴκου προστῆναι οὐκ οἶδεν, πῶς
ἐκκλησίας θεοῦ ἐπιμελήσεται;), [6]μὴ νεόφυτον, ἵνα μὴ τυφωθεὶς εἰς
κρίμα ἐμπέσῃ τοῦ διαβόλου. [7]δεῖ δὲ καὶ μαρτυρίαν καλὴν ἔχειν ἀπὸ
τῶν ἔξωθεν, ἵνα μὴ εἰς ὀνειδισμὸν ἐμπέσῃ καὶ παγίδα τοῦ διαβόλου.

Deacons

[8]Διακόνους ὡσαύτως σεμνούς, μὴ διλόγους, μὴ οἴνῳ πολλῷ
προσέχοντας, μὴ αἰσχροκερδεῖς, [9]ἔχοντας τὸ μυστήριον τῆς πίστεως
ἐν καθαρᾷ συνειδήσει. [10]καὶ οὗτοι δὲ δοκιμαζέσθωσαν πρῶτον, εἶτα
διακονείτωσαν ἀνέγκλητοι ὄντες. [11]Γυναῖκας ὡσαύτως σεμνάς, μὴ
διαβόλους, νηφαλίους, πιστὰς ἐν πᾶσιν. [12]διάκονοι ἔστωσαν μιᾶς
γυναικὸς ἄνδρες, τέκνων καλῶς προϊστάμενοι καὶ τῶν ἰδίων οἴκων.
[13]οἱ γὰρ καλῶς διακονήσαντες βαθμὸν ἑαυτοῖς καλὸν περιποιοῦνται
καὶ πολλὴν παρρησίαν ἐν πίστει τῇ ἐν Χριστῷ Ἰησοῦ.

God's Household & Its Head

[14]Ταῦτά σοι γράφω ἐλπίζων ἐλθεῖν πρὸς σὲ ἐν τάχει· [15]ἐὰν δὲ
βραδύνω, ἵνα εἰδῇς πῶς δεῖ ἐν οἴκῳ θεοῦ ἀναστρέφεσθαι, ἥτις ἐστὶν
ἐκκλησία θεοῦ ζῶντος, στῦλος καὶ ἑδραίωμα τῆς ἀληθείας. [16]καὶ
ὁμολογουμένως μέγα ἐστὶν τὸ τῆς εὐσεβείας μυστήριον·

3:16 The term *incontestably* is taken by a few witnesses as "we confess that." The earliest text evidently read *homologoumenōs*, which could be construed either as the adverb or as *homologoumen hōs* (initial *h* was not marked).

- **3:6** *Recent convert.* This is an obvious anachronism. In Paul's time all were neophytes. *Conceited* is applied to false teachers at 1 Tim 6:4; 2 Tim 3:4. The main purpose may be to suggest that those teachers win over only the inexperienced.
- **3:7** *Must.* Enjoying the approval of outsiders has moved from a desirable outcome to a necessity and is supplied with a purpose clause.
- **3:7** *Adversary's trap.* The meaning is not certain. It could refer to erring like the Devil or experiencing condemnation inflicted by the Devil.
- **3:8–13** The qualities expected of *deacons* match those of *bishops*, except for teaching, which is not a diaconal role.
- **3:9** *Revealed faith*, lit., "the mystery of faith." In the NT "mystery" often refers to divine secrets. In the context of "once hidden, now revealed," the translation is appropriate.
- **3:11** Women *deacons*. The word is *gynaikas*, which may mean "women" or "wives." Since the article is lacking and nothing is said of *bishops*' wives, this is the more probable meaning.
- **3:13** *Confidence.* This term has a long history in Greek thought. One element was freedom in speaking, even reckless abuse of rulers. Jews and Christians gave it an apocalyptic cast. The sense of self-assurance does not arise from recognition of one's own ability but from apprehension of divine love.
- **3:14–15** Brief travel plans, "apostolic parousia." These form a bracket with 4:13, marking the intervening material as a unit. Paul will be delayed, for-

5(Obviously, if someone doesn't know how to direct his own household, how will that person take care of the church of God?) 6The
bishop may not be a recent convert because of the danger that he
might become conceited and be tripped into condemnation by the
adversary. 7*Bishops* must enjoy a good reputation with outsiders to
avoid the danger of the adversary's trap and become an object of
derision.

Deacons

8Likewise, *deacons* must be sober, not insincere, not overly fond
of wine, nor out for shameful gain, 9maintaining the revealed faith
with a clear conscience. 10These persons must be evaluated and allowed to engage in service if they are beyond reproach. 11Women
deacons are to be sober, not slanderous, and temperate and reliable
in everything. 12Male *deacons* must not be married after a divorce,
must direct their children and household excellently. 13If they serve
well they will gain a good standing and substantial confidence in
their belief in the Anointed Jesus.

God's Household & Its Head

14As of this writing I hope to visit you presently, 15but if I am delayed, they will let you know how people are to behave in the household of God, which is the assembly of the living God, the pillar and
foundation of the truth. 16The essence of our revealed religion is incontestably majestic:

---

ever, but his legacy will replace physical presence.

• **3:16** That legacy is aptly summed up in a Christological hymn, examples of which from the Pauline tradition are Phil 2:6–11 and Col 1:15–20. Poetic features include Semitic structure of paired lines, as well as phonological and grammatical rhyming. The hymns have a creedal character.

The first pair moves from (evidently implied) pre-existence to incarnation, followed by vindication, not necessarily limited to resurrection in the sense of vivification of a corpse. The cause of justice is vindicated, not an individual person. Flesh and Spirit represent the natural and supernatural realms. The next couplet pairs revelation of Christ's victory in/to the celestial realm with the gentile mission. Mission is an extension of the resurrection. With the success of this mission (*embraced . . .*) Christ is permanently exalted. This conflates the Ascension of Acts 1 with the ultimate glorification. The Messianic mission is a there-and-back story. Its (unnamed) hero ends where he began. Still, the hymn is not merely sequential or biographical. *Revealed . . .* in line 3 does not simply refer to the angels at the empty tomb, who were subjects rather than recipients of revelation. The hymn is so non-concrete that it can receive myriad interpretations; it is exultant and mystical, but clearly focused on God's action for the world. The epiphany of the divine has stages, but it is a process rather than a dramatic reversal (e.g. death to resurrection), as in Philippians 2.

ὃς ἐφανερώθη ἐν σαρκί,
ἐδικαιώθη ἐν πνεύματι,
ὤφθη ἀγγέλοις,
ἐκηρύχθη ἐν ἔθνεσιν,
ἐπιστεύθη ἐν κόσμῳ,
ἀνελήμφθη ἐν δόξῃ.

Rival Teaching

4 Τὸ δὲ πνεῦμα ῥητῶς λέγει ὅτι ἐν ὑστέροις καιροῖς ἀποστήσονταί
τινες τῆς πίστεως προσέχοντες πνεύμασιν πλάνοις καὶ διδασκαλίαις
δαιμονίων, 2ἐν ὑποκρίσει ψευδολόγων, ἐκαυστηριασμένων τὴν
ἰδίαν συνείδησιν, 3κωλυόντων γαμεῖν, ἀπέχεσθαι βρωμάτων, ἃ
ὁ θεὸς ἔκτισεν εἰς μετάλημψιν μετὰ εὐχαριστίας τοῖς πιστοῖς καὶ
ἐπεγνωκόσι τὴν ἀλήθειαν. 4ὅτι πᾶν κτίσμα θεοῦ καλὸν καὶ οὐδὲν
ἀπόβλητον μετὰ εὐχαριστίας λαμβανόμενον· 5ἁγιάζεται γὰρ διὰ
λόγου θεοῦ καὶ ἐντεύξεως.

Timothy's Job Description

6Ταῦτα ὑποτιθέμενος τοῖς ἀδελφοῖς καλὸς ἔσῃ διάκονος Χριστοῦ
Ἰησοῦ, ἐντρεφόμενος τοῖς λόγοις τῆς πίστεως καὶ τῆς καλῆς
διδασκαλίας ᾗ παρηκολούθηκας· 7τοὺς δὲ βεβήλους καὶ γραώδεις
μύθους παραιτοῦ. Γύμναζε δὲ σεαυτὸν πρὸς εὐσέβειαν· 8ἡ γὰρ
σωματικὴ γυμνασία πρὸς ὀλίγον ἐστὶν ὠφέλιμος, ἡ δὲ εὐσέβεια πρὸς
πάντα ὠφέλιμός ἐστιν ἐπαγγελίαν ἔχουσα ζωῆς τῆς νῦν καὶ τῆς

- **4:1–5** The author provides some data about rivals, prefacing these with derogatory comments. Timothy has been warned previously, for false prophets are an indicator of the last days (Mark 13:22; 2 Thess 2:3; 1 John 2:18). This does not mean that the Pastor is claiming the nearness of the end. The last days (*critical moment*) are the interval between the two epiphanies of Christ. The source of the rival teaching is stigmatized as demonic; its human agents have defective moral awareness. The specifics (v. 3) are ascetic: abstention from sex and certain foods (probably meat). The historical Paul was unenthusiastic about marriage and dealt with dietary conflicts over food, most of Jewish origin, as pastoral issues. The opponents have reservations about the natural order, evidently generated by dualistic views opposing matter to spirit, and/or the belief that heavenly existence demands a vegetarian diet and the transcendence of sexual differentiation. They look to life before the Fall. The apostle and his converts in the Acts of Paul follow these principles. The Pastor responds with praise for creation and the claim that proper prayer over food removes any objection. He does not reject "meat sacrificed to idols," unlike Luke (Acts 15) and many others. Cf. Titus 1:14.

He was manifested in flesh,
vindicated in spirit,
revealed to heavenly messengers,
proclaimed among gentiles,
embraced throughout the world,
taken up in majesty.

Rival Teaching

4 Now the Spirit expressly says that at the critical moment some
will turn their backs on the faith by devoting themselves to deceiv-
ing spirits and demonic doctrines 2because of the pretentious dis-
semblance authorized by burned out consciences. 3They prohibit
marriage and demand abstention from foods that God created for
those who trust and who grasp what is true to eat with thanksgiving. 4Indeed, all that God has fashioned is good; nothing received
with thanksgiving is to be spurned. 5Petitions composed of divine
word render all foods sacred.

Timothy's Job Description

6If you promulgate these directives to the sisters and brothers,
you will be an excellent assistant of the Anointed Jesus, nourished
on the message of the faith and the excellent instruction that you
have followed. 7have nothing to do with vile old-wives' tales. Train
yourself in godliness. 8Now physical training is of limited value, but
godliness is of universal value, since it holds promise of existence
for both present and future. 9This is gospel truth that deserves un-

---

- **4:6–16** The Pastor sets out a proper lifestyle for leaders.
- **4:6** *Sisters and brothers*. Paul's generally egalitarian family language is rare in the PE, which prefer the model of a hierarchical family.
- **4:7** Improbable as it may seem, "old wives' tales" is a pejorative way of characterizing the rivals' legends, examples of which may be found in the Acts of Paul, notably the stories about Thecla (3–4).
- **4:7b–9** Since athletics (*ascēsis*, from which comes "asceticism") formed the core of the competitive Greek education of males, useful metaphors from gymnastic routines entered the vocabulary. (Cf. the "exercises" found in language and other areas of study, as well as "spiritual exercises.") On the other hand, popular philosophy regarded the pursuit of buff bodies and transitory glory as a waste. The Pastor utilizes that anti-gymnasium tradition. This proverb aptly contrasts Christianity with the anti-intellectual bent of the general culture, allying it instead with moral philosophy.

μελλούσης. 9πιστὸς ὁ λόγος καὶ πάσης ἀποδοχῆς ἄξιος· 10εἰς τοῦτο γὰρ κοπιῶμεν καὶ ἀγωνιζόμεθα, ὅτι ἠλπίκαμεν ἐπὶ θεῷ ζῶντι, ὅς ἐστιν σωτὴρ πάντων ἀνθρώπων μάλιστα πιστῶν.

11Παράγγελλε ταῦτα καὶ δίδασκε. 12Μηδείς σου τῆς νεότητος καταφρονείτω, ἀλλὰ τύπος γίνου τῶν πιστῶν ἐν λόγῳ, ἐν ἀναστροφῇ, ἐν ἀγάπῃ, ἐν πίστει, ἐν ἁγνείᾳ. 13ἕως ἔρχομαι πρόσεχε τῇ ἀναγνώσει, τῇ παρακλήσει, τῇ διδασκαλίᾳ. 14μὴ ἀμέλει τοῦ ἐν σοὶ χαρίσματος, ὃ ἐδόθη σοι διὰ προφητείας μετὰ ἐπιθέσεως τῶν χειρῶν τοῦ πρεσβυτερίου. 15ταῦτα μελέτα, ἐν τούτοις ἴσθι, ἵνα σου ἡ προκοπὴ φανερὰ ᾖ πᾶσιν. 16ἔπεχε σεαυτῷ καὶ τῇ διδασκαλίᾳ, ἐπίμενε αὐτοῖς· τοῦτο γὰρ ποιῶν καὶ σεαυτὸν σώσεις καὶ τοὺς ἀκούοντάς σου.

Rules for Age Groups

5 Πρεσβυτέρῳ μὴ ἐπιπλήξῃς ἀλλὰ παρακάλει ὡς πατέρα, νεωτέρους ὡς ἀδελφούς, 2πρεσβυτέρας ὡς μητέρας, νεωτέρας ὡς ἀδελφὰς ἐν πάσῃ ἁγνείᾳ.

Widows

3Χήρας τίμα τὰς ὄντως χήρας. 4εἰ δέ τις χήρα τέκνα ἢ ἔκγονα ἔχει, μανθανέτωσαν πρῶτον τὸν ἴδιον οἶκον εὐσεβεῖν καὶ ἀμοιβὰς

4:10 A somewhat less well-attested variant to *struggle* is "we are reproached." This is the more difficult reading and may be preferable.
4:14 A few good witnesses correct *council of presbyters* to "a presbyter." The difference is one letter. The "presbytery" is rare but certainly correct.

- **4:10** Apostolic labor does not take place in the gym for short periods. It is tough, gritty, unending toil.
- **4:11–16** Rules for young pastors. The fiction of Timothy's youth and his inexperience justifies the publication of guides. Timothy is to lead by example, a principle of enduring merit. The essence of pastoral care can be summed up as a range of verbal activities, to which perseverance and suffering are added.
- **4:12** Ignatius urges the Magnesians not to take advantage of the youth of bishop Damas, IgnMag 3.
- **4:13** Reading aloud required practice and skill, for manuscripts were all unspaced capitals: GODISNOWHERE.
- **4:14** This describes an ordination. On the prophetic element cf. Acts 13:1–3 and the comments upon Titus 1:18. Combined with 2 Tim 1:6, one observes the emerging model. This ceremony imparts a spiritual gift (*charisma*) and is thus more than authorization or commission. For the pastor the gift is a resource.
- **4:16** The basics were behavior, including care of self, and belief. Correlation between policy and practice, deeds and words, was a fundamental test for ancient thought systems and permeates early Christian thought.

qualified acceptance. [10]This is why we toil and struggle, because our confidence is lodged in the living God, who is the liberator of all people, especially the believers.

[11]Proclaim and teach the aforesaid. [12]Don't let anyone make an issue of your youth; rather serve as an example for the believers in speech, conduct, love, trust in God, and holiness. [13]Apply yourself to public reading, exhortation, and instruction until I get there. [14]Do not overlook the gift within you, that conveyed through the council of presbyters through the imposition of hands after prophetic authorization. [15]Make these things your constant occupation; center yourself within them, so that your growth will be apparent to everyone. [16]Be persistently attentive to yourself and to your teaching, for by so doing you will keep both yourself and your hearers in good spiritual health.

Rules for Age Groups

5 Do not upbraid an elderly man; rather advise him as you would a father. Respond to younger men as to brothers. [2]Similarly, treat elderly women as mothers and younger women as sisters—the latter with utmost discretion.

Widows

[3]As for widows, genuine widows deserve support. [4]If a widow has children or grandchildren, they must first learn to show proper rev-

---

- **5:1–6:2** continue discussion of the Household of God, commingling church and domestic structure. Chap. 5 returns to the theme of Church Order, ending with instructions for Timothy, "the bishop," for managing clergy and, like chap. 4, with reflections on self-care. Once again, women agitate the Pastor. Regarding the elderly and young the Pastor has two verses of sound advice; widows merit fourteen.
- **5:3–16** *Widows.* These fall into groups. Vv. 3–8 deal with the support of widows. Vv. 9–15 discuss the order of widows, with attention to both qualifications and duties. V. 16 frames the unit. The existence of a large number of widows indicates a community of considerable size. Widows were numerous both because of high mortality and the tendency toward age disparity. Mature men married girls. (Frequent pregnancy and childbirth struck down many women; widowers would often marry young women, who might become widows.)
- **5:3–8** The Pastor has two concerns: money and behavior. Support of widows placed a burden upon the community. Whenever possible (presumably believing), relatives should provide support. V. 8 classifies failure to do so as tantamount to apostasy. Charity begins at home. Proper widows should act like widows. Merry widows deserve no aid. Anna (Luke 2:36–37) is the kind of widow of whom the Pastor approves.

ἀποδιδόναι τοῖς προγόνοις· τοῦτο γάρ ἐστιν ἀπόδεκτον ἐνώπιον
τοῦ θεοῦ. 5ἡ δὲ ὄντως χήρα καὶ μεμονωμένη ἤλπικεν ἐπὶ θεὸν καὶ
προσμένει ταῖς δεήσεσιν καὶ ταῖς προσευχαῖς νυκτὸς καὶ ἡμέρας,
6ἡ δὲ σπαταλῶσα ζῶσα τέθνηκεν. 7καὶ ταῦτα παράγγελλε, ἵνα
ἀνεπίλημπτοι ὦσιν.

Relatives

8εἰ δέ τις τῶν ἰδίων καὶ μάλιστα οἰκείων οὐ προνοεῖ, τὴν πίστιν
ἤρνηται καὶ ἔστιν ἀπίστου χείρων.

Order of Widows

9Χήρα καταλεγέσθω μὴ ἔλαττον

ἐτῶν ἑξήκοντα γεγονυῖα,
ἑνὸς ἀνδρὸς γυνή,
10ἐν ἔργοις καλοῖς μαρτυρουμένη,
εἰ ἐτεκνοτρόφησεν,
εἰ ἐξενοδόχησεν,
εἰ ἁγίων πόδας ἔνιψεν,
εἰ θλιβομένοις ἐπήρκεσεν,
εἰ παντὶ ἔργῳ ἀγαθῷ ἐπηκολούθησεν.

11νεωτέρας δὲ χήρας παραιτοῦ· ὅταν γὰρ καταστρηνιάσωσιν τοῦ
Χριστοῦ, γαμεῖν θέλουσιν 12ἔχουσαι κρίμα ὅτι τὴν πρώτην πίστιν
ἠθέτησαν· 13ἅμα δὲ καὶ ἀργαὶ μανθάνουσιν περιερχόμεναι τὰς οἰκίας,
οὐ μόνον δὲ ἀργαὶ ἀλλὰ καὶ φλύαροι καὶ περίεργοι, λαλοῦσαι τὰ μὴ
δέοντα.

14Βούλομαι οὖν νεωτέρας γαμεῖν, τεκνογονεῖν, οἰκοδεσποτεῖν,
μηδεμίαν ἀφορμὴν διδόναι τῷ ἀντικειμένῳ λοιδορίας χάριν· 15ἤδη
γάρ τινες ἐξετράπησαν ὀπίσω τοῦ σατανᾶ. 16εἴ τις πιστὴ ἔχει χήρας,
ἐπαρκείτω αὐταῖς καὶ μὴ βαρείσθω ἡ ἐκκλησία, ἵνα ταῖς ὄντως
χήραις ἐπαρκέσῃ.

Presbyters

17Οἱ καλῶς προεστῶτες πρεσβύτεροι διπλῆς τιμῆς ἀξιούσθωσαν,
μάλιστα οἱ κοπιῶντες ἐν λόγῳ καὶ διδασκαλίᾳ. 18λέγει γὰρ ἡ γραφή·

- **5:9–16** The order is an organized body of women who make lifelong commitments (v. 12). They are discussed with the officers. Although called "widows," the body may have sometimes included a range of unmarried women. Rules regarding age and parenthood would exclude those not technically widows. Acts 9:36–43 reflects such a body, supported by the patronage of Tabitha. Acts 6:1–2 shows that readers would not be surprised to learn that widows could raise loud and clear complaints. They did; for centuries widows made bishops earn their pay. Their duties include ministering to the sick and needy and providing hospitality. The last was a crucial component of early Christian mission and networking. These duties involved leaving the home; elderly women were both experienced in care-giving and unlikely to generate suspicions of impropriety. Entrée to various households concerns the Pastor, for hospitality may be given to travelers of whom he does not ap-

erence for their own family and to give back to their forebears, for
this is pleasing to God. 5The genuine widow is all alone and places her
hope in God. She is constant in supplication and prayer, night and
day. 6The indulgent widow, by contrast, might as well be dead. 7Make
these instructions clear so that the widows might be irreproachable.

Relatives

8Whoever does not care for their own people—especially family
members—amounts to an apostate and is worse than a non-believer.

Order of Widows

9No widow is to be enrolled on the register unless she

is at least sixty;
is not a remarried divorcée;
10is attested by good works;
has children;
exhibited hospitality;
performed menial services for believers;
succored those in distress;
in general, pursued every kind of excellent activity.

11Do not enroll younger widows. When passion takes priority over
Christ, they will wish to marry and 12be liable to the charge of for-
saking their first commitment. 13These idle creatures will develop
the habit of flitting from house to house, filling empty hours with
gossip and meddling, saying things best left unsaid.

14For these reasons I want younger widows to marry, have children and be homemakers, providing opponents with no occasions
to abuse us. 15The fact is that some women have already become followers of Satan. 16If a woman believer has widows in her household,
she is to care for them and not burden the church, so that it can care
for the genuine widows.

Presbyters

17*Presbyters* who manage well deserve double remuneration, especially those who labor intensely in preaching and teaching, 18for
Scripture says: "Don't muzzle threshing oxen," and "Workers de-

---

prove and widows may circulate ideas and stories that are not to his liking. Cf. 2 Tim 3:6. 1 Tim 3:14–15 raise appropriate surface concerns for guardians of the church's honor, but they also view the order of widows as a potential nursery of heresy and individuals as possible Janey Appleseeds who might plant those seedlings widely.

- **5:9** *Sixty* was the general mark of "old age."
- **5:17–25** The regulations for presbyters envision Timothy as the single supervisor of presbyters.
- **5:17–18** treat what is now called "clergy compensation." At least some presbyters have supervisory responsibilities, perhaps over a house church. (The verb *manage* is applied both to the community and to households, as

βοῦν ἀλοῶντα οὐ φιμώσεις, καί· ἄξιος ὁ ἐργάτης τοῦ μισθοῦ αὐτοῦ.
[19]κατὰ πρεσβυτέρου κατηγορίαν μὴ παραδέχου, ἐκτὸς εἰ μὴ ἐπὶ δύο ἢ
τριῶν μαρτύρων. [20]Τοὺς ἁμαρτάνοντας ἐνώπιον πάντων ἔλεγχε, ἵνα
καὶ οἱ λοιποὶ φόβον ἔχωσιν.

[21]Διαμαρτύρομαι ἐνώπιον τοῦ θεοῦ καὶ Χριστοῦ Ἰησοῦ καὶ τῶν
ἐκλεκτῶν ἀγγέλων, ἵνα ταῦτα φυλάξῃς χωρὶς προκρίματος, μηδὲν
ποιῶν κατὰ πρόσκλισιν. [22]χεῖρας ταχέως μηδενὶ ἐπιτίθει μηδὲ
κοινώνει ἁμαρτίαις ἀλλοτρίαις· σεαυτὸν ἁγνὸν τήρει.

[23]Μηκέτι ὑδροπότει, ἀλλὰ οἴνῳ ὀλίγῳ χρῶ διὰ τὸν στόμαχον καὶ
τὰς πυκνάς σου ἀσθενείας.

[24]Τινῶν ἀνθρώπων αἱ ἁμαρτίαι πρόδηλοί εἰσιν προάγουσαι εἰς
κρίσιν, τισὶν δὲ καὶ ἐπακολουθοῦσιν· [25]ὡσαύτως καὶ τὰ ἔργα τὰ καλὰ
πρόδηλα, καὶ τὰ ἄλλως ἔχοντα κρυβῆναι οὐ δύνανται.

Slaves

6 Ὅσοι εἰσὶν ὑπὸ ζυγὸν δοῦλοι, τοὺς ἰδίους δεσπότας πάσης τιμῆς
ἀξίους ἡγείσθωσαν, ἵνα μὴ τὸ ὄνομα τοῦ θεοῦ καὶ ἡ διδασκαλία
βλασφημῆται. [2]οἱ δὲ πιστοὺς ἔχοντες δεσπότας μὴ καταφρονείτωσαν,
ὅτι ἀδελφοί εἰσιν, ἀλλὰ μᾶλλον δουλευέτωσαν, ὅτι πιστοί εἰσιν καὶ
ἀγαπητοὶ οἱ τῆς εὐεργεσίας ἀντιλαμβανόμενοι. Ταῦτα δίδασκε καὶ
παρακάλει.

5:19 Part of the D-Text tradition omits *without two or three witnesses.* This may reflect debates about canon law.

---

in 1 Tim 3:4, 5, 12.) The *remuneration* may amount to no more than a double portion of food at common meals (the *agapē*), which could feed one for the next day. Support for this comes from 1 Cor 9:9. Readers are evidently expected to know 1 Cor 9:9–14, that is, the figurative interpretation of the ox-saying. Rather than Paul's general appeal in v. 14, however, the Pastor can now quote Luke 10:7. Both are labeled "scripture," authoritative writing. See "Scripture," p. 66.

- **5:19–21** take up ecclesiastical discipline. Accusations require a minimum of two witnesses. Cf. Deuteronomy 19 and Matthew 18. This protects presbyters against wild or unfounded accusations but rules out misconduct against an individual in private. Since rebuke is the only sanction, the faults in view must be minor. The motive for public correction is not transparency but creation of an atmosphere of fear. V. 21 contains typical warnings to those in supervisory roles.
- **5:21** The triad, "God, Christ, angels," in traditional language, may have an eschatological origin: Christ coming with angels in the glory of the Father. Cf. Luke 9:26. This is effectively a reminder of judgment.
- **5:22–23** engage the personal. Favoritism might lead to premature ordination. This leads the Pastor to note the dangers that can arise, often inadvertently, from associations. Then comes a "twofer." The admonition to take a drop or two from time to time is an indirect blow to ascetic rivals and a

serve to be paid." [19]Do not entertain an accusation against a *presbyter* without two or three witnesses. [20]Rebuke wrongdoers publicly, so that others may learn respect.

[21]I adjure you that, before God, the Anointed Jesus, and the elect celestial beings, you observe these directives without prejudice, avoiding any hint of partiality. [22]Ordain no one without time for examination and preparation; do not get entangled in the errors of others. Stay aloof from evil.

[23]Stop teetotaling; a little wine will aid your digestion and your recurrent maladies.

[24]Some people's sins are conspicuous, preceding them to condemnation; others' failures only catch up with them later. [25]Good deeds are no less conspicuous; bad actions cannot remain concealed.

Slaves

6 Let all the enslaved regard their particular owners as deserving of complete respect, so that God's name and our doctrine may not be reviled. [2]Moreover those with believing owners are not to be contemptuous of them on the grounds that they are brothers or sisters—they should be even more abject slaves because their owners devote themselves to beneficent deeds and are beloved believers. Teach these principles and encourage obedience.

---

trope for self-care, which is important for the care of others.

- **5:24–25** are consolatory. The truth will out. As always, the public image of the church is vital to its mission (which includes its security).
- **6** The structure of chap. 6 is difficult. See "The Structure of 1 Timothy," p. 32. The first two verses finish up comments on social groups, with clear intimations that slaves are prone to unsound views, leading to a denunciation of those views that provides an overture to discussion of the problems of money. A creedal and doxological statement is followed by a return to the subject of wealth, and a brief closing charge. 1 Timothy is like an ordination sermon with several goals. One is the nature of ministry and its place within the structure of the church. Another is the character and duties of the ordinand. Furthermore, there is the body of the faithful, in need of edification. The preacher wisely does not address these in turn, but moves back and forth among them, but with little artistry, leaving hearers a bit discontented, if not confused.
- **6:1–2** The Pastor has nothing positive for slaves. They hope in vain for emancipation and recognition of their Christian status.
- **6:2** An alternate translation is "[Masters] who benefit by kindnesses." This is less likely because the noun *euergesia* (benefaction) belongs to the realm of *noblesse oblige* and flows down rather than up the social ladder. The argument is that slave owners discharge their Christian duty by a range of good works rather than by favoring their slaves.

Unsound Belief

3εἴ τις ἑτεροδιδασκαλεῖ καὶ μὴ προσέρχεται ὑγιαίνουσιν λόγοις
τοῖς τοῦ κυρίου ἡμῶν Ἰησοῦ Χριστοῦ καὶ τῇ κατ᾽ εὐσέβειαν
διδασκαλίᾳ, 4τετύφωται, μηδὲν ἐπιστάμενος, ἀλλὰ νοσῶν περὶ
ζητήσεις καὶ λογομαχίας, ἐξ ὧν γίνεται φθόνος ἔρις βλασφημίαι,
ὑπόνοιαι πονηραί, 5διαπαρατριβαὶ διεφθαρμένων ἀνθρώπων τὸν
νοῦν καὶ ἀπεστερημένων τῆς ἀληθείας, νομιζόντων πορισμὸν εἶναι
τὴν εὐσέβειαν.

Wealth & Competition

6Ἔστιν δὲ πορισμὸς μέγας ἡ εὐσέβεια μετὰ αὐταρκείας·

7οὐδὲν γὰρ εἰσηνέγκαμεν εἰς τὸν κόσμον,
ὅτι οὐδὲ ἐξενεγκεῖν τι δυνάμεθα·
8ἔχοντες δὲ διατροφὰς καὶ σκεπάσματα,
τούτοις ἀρκεσθησόμεθα.

9οἱ δὲ βουλόμενοι πλουτεῖν ἐμπίπτουσιν εἰς πειρασμὸν καὶ παγίδα
καὶ ἐπιθυμίας πολλὰς ἀνοήτους καὶ βλαβεράς, αἵτινες βυθίζουσιν
τοὺς ἀνθρώπους εἰς ὄλεθρον καὶ ἀπώλειαν· 10ῥίζα γὰρ πάντων τῶν
κακῶν ἐστιν ἡ φιλαργυρία, ἧς τινες ὀρεγόμενοι ἀπεπλανήθησαν
ἀπὸ τῆς πίστεως καὶ ἑαυτοὺς περιέπειραν ὀδύναις πολλαῖς.
11Σὺ δέ, ὦ ἄνθρωπε θεοῦ, ταῦτα φεῦγε·

δίωκε δὲ δικαιοσύνην εὐσέβειαν πίστιν, ἀγάπην ὑπομονὴν
πραϋπαθίαν.
12ἀγωνίζου τὸν καλὸν ἀγῶνα τῆς πίστεως,

ἐπιλαβοῦ τῆς αἰωνίου ζωῆς, εἰς ἣν ἐκλήθης καὶ ὡμολόγησας
τὴν καλὴν ὁμολογίαν ἐνώπιον πολλῶν μαρτύρων. 13παραγγέλλω

6:5 An example of the pedantry of the D-Text is the addition of "stay away from people like that."

- **6:3–5** Rivals get character-assassination with an anti-intellectual twist. The Pastor will not or cannot teach Timothy how to engage in debate; his depressing solution is to shun opponents and avoid argument. V. 4 represents the health imagery used to characterize teaching. See 1:10 and "Sound Teaching," p. 33. The catalogue of vv. 4–5 is oriented to sources of division. This is a common political tactic: "Those who do not agree with me are fomenting division." The charge that they are out for gain is also standard.
- **6:6–8** The next subject is apt for benefactors. The Pastor promotes a doctrine promoted by Cynics and Stoics: Don't be owned by possessions. The less we need the freer and more secure we are. As v. 6 intimates, social climbing is undesirable. The construction of the commonplace in v. 7 is diffi-

Unsound Belief

[3]Whoever teaches otherwise and does not adhere to the wholesome message of our master Jesus Christ and the doctrine befit-
ting true religion [4]is swollen with conceit, utterly ignorant, driven
instead by a pathological interest in research and disputes about
terms, which lead to envy, conflict, slanders, malicious suspicions,
[5]in short, the abrasive wranglings of warped minds denuded of
truth, what one expects from people who view religion as a source
of gain.

Wealth & Competition

[6]Religion actually does produce a large profit, for it teaches how
to manage with what one has.

> [7]Since we brought nothing into this world,
> we cannot transport anything out of it.
> [8]If we have food and covering,
> we shall be content.

[9]Those, however, who want to get rich are stumbling into a
tempting trap and many baneful cravings that plunge people into
ruinous destruction, [10]for the pursuit of wealth is the root of all evil.
Aspiring for wealth has led many away from the faith and caused
them to inflict woes upon themselves.

[11]On the contrary, godly person, flee these things.

> Pursue justice, piety, trust, love, patient endurance, and
> gentleness.
> [12]Compete in the noble struggle of faith;

Lay hold of unbounded existence, to which you were called and made the noble declaration in the presence of numerous wit-

---

cult. It should be concessive, as here translated *since we . . . we cannot, . . .* but the syntax is cloudy.

- **6:10** is a common proverb. It should be contrasted with its short form, for the proverb does *not* say that money is the root of all evil. PolPhil 4:1 also cites this insight.
- **6:11–15** Now comes the corresponding list of virtues. These verses apply to all, not just leaders like Timothy. This closing shows the Pastor at his best. Note the parallel between the confession of Jesus before Pilate and that of the faithful, vv. 13–14 (Luke 23:3 may be the source of the former). After climaxing, appropriately, with a reference to the final epiphany, comes a soaring doxology, stressing the power and transcendence of God.

[σοι] ἐνώπιον τοῦ θεοῦ τοῦ ζῳογονοῦντος τὰ πάντα καὶ Χριστοῦ
Ἰησοῦ τοῦ μαρτυρήσαντος ἐπὶ Ποντίου Πιλάτου τὴν καλὴν
ὁμολογίαν, 14τηρῆσαί σε τὴν ἐντολὴν ἄσπιλον ἀνεπίλημπτον μέχρι
τῆς ἐπιφανείας τοῦ κυρίου ἡμῶν Ἰησοῦ Χριστοῦ, 15ἣν καιροῖς ἰδίοις
δείξει

ὁ μακάριος καὶ μόνος δυνάστης,
ὁ βασιλεὺς τῶν βασιλευόντων καὶ κύριος τῶν κυριευόντων,
16ὁ μόνος ἔχων ἀθανασίαν,
φῶς οἰκῶν ἀπρόσιτον,
ὃν εἶδεν οὐδεὶς ἀνθρώπων οὐδὲ ἰδεῖν δύναται·
ᾧ τιμὴ καὶ κράτος αἰώνιον, ἀμήν.

17Τοῖς πλουσίοις ἐν τῷ νῦν αἰῶνι παράγγελλε μὴ ὑψηλοφρονεῖν
μηδὲ ἠλπικέναι ἐπὶ πλούτου ἀδηλότητι ἀλλ᾽ ἐπὶ θεῷ τῷ
παρέχοντι ἡμῖν πάντα πλουσίως εἰς ἀπόλαυσιν, 18ἀγαθοεργεῖν,
πλουτεῖν ἐν ἔργοις καλοῖς, εὐμεταδότους εἶναι, κοινωνικούς,
19ἀποθησαυρίζοντας ἑαυτοῖς θεμέλιον καλὸν εἰς τὸ μέλλον, ἵνα
ἐπιλάβωνται τῆς ὄντως ζωῆς.

Epistolary Close

20Ὦ Τιμόθεε, τὴν παραθήκην φύλαξον ἐκτρεπόμενος τὰς
βεβήλους κενοφωνίας καὶ ἀντιθέσεις τῆς ψευδωνύμου γνώσεως,
21ἥν τινες ἐπαγγελλόμενοι περὶ τὴν πίστιν ἠστόχησαν.

Ἡ χάρις μεθ᾽ ὑμῶν.

6:19 The Byzantine text replaces *genuine* with the more conventional "eternal," another typical change.
6:21 Byzantine and other witnesses change *you all* to the singular. This fits the ostensible audience (Timothy).

Increasingly more elaborate subscriptions offer details about the author and place of composition.

- **6:17–19** This dreadful anti-climax (perhaps inspired by Luke 12:16–21) defies explanation.
- **6:20–21a** The exhortation to guard the deposit forms a bracket with 1:3. Community protection is the goal. Servant three in the Parable of the Talents (Matt 25:14–30) is now deserving of all praise. The final hit at the

nesses. [13]I charge you, before the God who gives everything life and
the Anointed Jesus who made the noble declaration before Pontius
Pilate, [14]to keep the commandment without tarnish or blame until
the appearance of our master Jesus Christ, [15]which God will usher in
at the judicious moment—

God, the felicitous and unique sovereign,
greatest of monarchs and mightiest of rulers,
[16]who alone possesses freedom from death,
who resides in light unapproachable;
whom no mortal has seen or could see.
To God be honor and endless dominion. Amen.

[17]Advise those who are rich from the worldly perspective not to
be proud of their status, nor to lodge their expectations with uncertain wealth, but rather with God, who generously endows us with
all that we need to enjoy life. [18]Urge them to do good, to exhibit a
wealth of good deeds, to promote the common good generously,
[19]storing up thereby a fine basis for their future possession of genuine existence.

Epistolary Close

[20]My dear Timothy, protect what has been entrusted. Steer clear of vulgar and vacuous chatter and the contradictions of what is
wrongly labeled knowledge. [21]Adherence to this has led some to deviate from the faith.

Grace be with you all.

---

opponents contains two intriguing terms: *contradictions* corresponds to the method of Marcion, and the title of one of his books. *Wrongly labeled knowledge* so suited Irenaeus as a derogation of systems he attacked that he included the phrase in the long title of his *Against the Heresies* (c. 180). 1 Timothy apparently shows that these words were beginning to acquire a distinct coloration.

- **6:21b** The closing greeting is very brief, suitable to a text that only existed as part of a collection.

2 TIMOTHY

Epistolary Opening

1 Παῦλος ἀπόστολος Χριστοῦ Ἰησοῦ διὰ θελήματος θεοῦ κατ᾽
ἐπαγγελίαν ζωῆς τῆς ἐν Χριστῷ Ἰησοῦ [2]Τιμοθέῳ ἀγαπητῷ τέκνῳ,
χάρις ἔλεος εἰρήνη ἀπὸ θεοῦ πατρὸς καὶ Χριστοῦ Ἰησοῦ τοῦ κυρίου
ἡμῶν.

Thanksgiving

[3]Χάριν ἔχω τῷ θεῷ, ᾧ λατρεύω ἀπὸ προγόνων ἐν καθαρᾷ
συνειδήσει, ὡς ἀδιάλειπτον ἔχω τὴν περὶ σοῦ μνείαν ἐν ταῖς
δεήσεσίν μου νυκτὸς καὶ ἡμέρας, [4]ἐπιποθῶν σε ἰδεῖν, μεμνημένος
σου τῶν δακρύων, ἵνα χαρᾶς πληρωθῶ, [5]ὑπόμνησιν λαβὼν τῆς ἐν
σοὶ ἀνυποκρίτου πίστεως, ἥτις ἐνῴκησεν πρῶτον ἐν τῇ μάμμῃ σου
Λωΐδι καὶ τῇ μητρί σου Εὐνίκῃ, πέπεισμαι δὲ ὅτι καὶ ἐν σοί.

Timothy's Vocation

[6]Δι᾽ ἣν αἰτίαν ἀναμιμνῄσκω σε ἀναζωπυρεῖν τὸ χάρισμα τοῦ
θεοῦ, ὅ ἐστιν ἐν σοὶ διὰ τῆς ἐπιθέσεως τῶν χειρῶν μου. [7]οὐ γὰρ
ἔδωκεν ἡμῖν ὁ θεὸς πνεῦμα δειλίας ἀλλὰ δυνάμεως καὶ ἀγάπης καὶ
σωφρονισμοῦ. [8]μὴ οὖν ἐπαισχυνθῇς τὸ μαρτύριον τοῦ κυρίου ἡμῶν
μηδὲ ἐμὲ τὸν δέσμιον αὐτοῦ, ἀλλὰ συγκακοπάθησον τῷ εὐαγγελίῳ
κατὰ δύναμιν θεοῦ,

• **2 Timothy** has a different formal character from the other PE, for it takes on many features of the Testament genre, the last words of a dying man. This genre allowed for a good deal of advice to the subsequent generation. Part of its appeal lies in the enduring respect for a person's last wishes. To this may be added the emotional appeal of pathos. The milieu of 2 Timothy is quite similar to Acts 20:17–38, Paul's farewell to the presbyters of Ephesus. That speech may well have helped inspire this letter.

The author does an effective job of correlating, in true Pauline fashion, the mission and suffering of Jesus with the life of the apostle and of his successors. Paul, like Jesus, dies abandoned and deserted. This builds to a climax in the peroration, which remains powerful despite what strikes many readers of today as excessive pathos. Luke daubed on his pathos with a trowel; the Pastor does not hesitate to use a shovel.

The body (1:6–4:18) has a perceptible structure:

I. 1:6–8 Timothy's vocation (A)
   1:9–18 Paul's suffering and experience, with creed (B)
   2:1–7 Timothy's vocation (A)
   2:8–13 Suffering, with creed (B)
II. 2:14–3:9 Rival Teaching

Epistolary Opening

1 Paul, an envoy of the Anointed Jesus through the resolution of
God and the concomitant promise of life in the Anointed Jesus: [2]to
my beloved child Timothy: Favor, compassion and wellbeing from
our fatherly God and the Anointed Jesus our master.

Thanksgiving

[3]I thank God, whom, following my ancestors, I worship with a
clear conscience, when I remember you in my prayers, as I unceas-
ingly do, day and night. [4]When I remember your tears I long to see
you, so that I may be filled with joy, [5]as I recall your unfeigned trust,
which dwelt first with your grandmother Lois, then your mother
Eunice, and assuredly also in you.

Timothy's Vocation

[6]That is why I remind you to fan the flames of the heavenly gift
that is in you through the laying on of my hands, [7]for God's spirit
does not bestow cowardice upon us, but power, affection, and good
sense. [8]Therefore don't be offended by what is said about our master
or me, his prisoner, but accept your part of suffering on behalf of the
great message, as you receive power from God,

III. 3:10–13 Paul's Suffering (B)
  3:14–4:5 Timothy's vocation (A)
IV. 4:6–18 Peroration

- **1:1–2** This is a standard opening to a Pauline letter.
- **1:3–5** As in Paul, the thanksgiving can intimate major themes, here Paul as a model of fidelity and Timothy as a bearer of tradition. The three generations depicted indicate the framework of the household of God, the perspective of three Christian generations, and women as nurturers of faith. This is at variance with Acts 16:1–3. Like Acts, the Pastor opposes Jewish beliefs but utilizes Jewish ancestry and scripture to show continuity.
- **1:6–8** This vivid imagery (inspired by the Pentecost fire of Acts 2?) is more effective than an appeal to memory. "Use what you have" is always good advice. No less effective is the language used to say that the spirit bestows courage. This aptly introduces the Christological warrant. Jesus died a disreputable death, and I am headed for the chopping block. The Pastor and all martyrs keep alive the flame of hope that has turned the world upside down and inverted the exquisitely crafted apparatus of honor and shame. In contrast to 1 Tim 4:14, v. 6 appears to envision Paul alone as ordaining Timothy.

Paul's Suffering & Experience

[9]τοῦ σώσαντος ἡμᾶς
καὶ καλέσαντος κλήσει ἁγίᾳ,
οὐ κατὰ τὰ ἔργα ἡμῶν
ἀλλὰ κατὰ ἰδίαν πρόθεσιν καὶ χάριν,
τὴν δοθεῖσαν ἡμῖν ἐν Χριστῷ Ἰησοῦ πρὸ χρόνων αἰωνίων,
[10]φανερωθεῖσαν δὲ νῦν
διὰ τῆς ἐπιφανείας τοῦ σωτῆρος ἡμῶν Χριστοῦ Ἰησοῦ,
καταργήσαντος μὲν τὸν θάνατον
φωτίσαντος δὲ ζωὴν καὶ ἀφθαρσίαν διὰ τοῦ εὐαγγελίου

[11]εἰς ὃ ἐτέθην ἐγὼ κῆρυξ καὶ ἀπόστολος καὶ διδάσκαλος, [12]δι'
ἣν αἰτίαν καὶ ταῦτα πάσχω· ἀλλ' οὐκ ἐπαισχύνομαι, οἶδα γὰρ ᾧ
πεπίστευκα καὶ πέπεισμαι ὅτι δυνατός ἐστιν τὴν παραθήκην μου
φυλάξαι εἰς ἐκείνην τὴν ἡμέραν. [13]Ὑποτύπωσιν ἔχε ὑγιαινόντων
λόγων ὧν παρ' ἐμοῦ ἤκουσας ἐν πίστει καὶ ἀγάπῃ τῇ ἐν Χριστῷ
Ἰησοῦ· [14]τὴν καλὴν παραθήκην φύλαξον διὰ πνεύματος ἁγίου τοῦ
ἐνοικοῦντος ἐν ἡμῖν.

[15]Οἶδας τοῦτο, ὅτι ἀπεστράφησάν με πάντες οἱ ἐν τῇ Ἀσίᾳ, ὧν
ἐστιν Φύγελος καὶ Ἑρμογένης. [16]δῴη ἔλεος ὁ κύριος τῷ Ὀνησιφόρου
οἴκῳ, ὅτι πολλάκις με ἀνέψυξεν καὶ τὴν ἅλυσίν μου οὐκ ἐπαισχύνθη,
[17]ἀλλὰ γενόμενος ἐν Ῥώμῃ σπουδαίως ἐζήτησέν με καὶ εὗρεν· [18]δῴη
αὐτῷ ὁ κύριος εὑρεῖν ἔλεος παρὰ κυρίου ἐν ἐκείνῃ τῇ ἡμέρᾳ. καὶ ὅσα
ἐν Ἐφέσῳ διηκόνησεν, βέλτιον σὺ γινώσκεις.

1:11 Most witnesses add "of gentiles" to *instructor*. This may be a harmonization from 1 Tim 2:7.

- **1:9–10** The reference to the power of the gospel appositely introduces a creedal declaration, probably based upon traditional phrases. This hymn-like formula approximates the figure of "climax," in which the predicate of each clause becomes subject of the next. The unit is built upon two antitheses. The first is that salvation is not earned but given. The Pastor holds the necessity of good works but rejects them as means for meriting deliverance. The second contrasts the "once" of darkness and mortality to the "now" of immortality and light. By these means the Pastor fits the "once . . . now" eschatological formula into his epiphany model. "Immortality" is not a Pauline or primitive Christian concept. Note that the cross is not mentioned. "Atonement" means the destruction of death's power.
- **1:10** *Deliverer*. The title "savior" is not found in the earliest Christological statements. In the PE it corresponds to ruler cult usage.
- **1:11–12** fashion the passage into an A B A statement.
- **1:11** For Paul "agent" (apostle) sufficed. *Herald* appears c. 100 in Christian writings. This has a sacral sense. Paul brings the official announcement from God. *Teacher* has now assumed such prominence that it appears on

Paul's Suffering and Experience

[9]who rescued us
and invited us with a godly summons
not in response to what we have achieved,
but through God's own purpose and generosity,
bestowed upon us by the Anointed Jesus before time,
[10]but now made visible
through the arrival of our deliverer the Anointed Jesus,
who has terminated death's power
and brought true and boundless existence to light, through
the great message.

[11]For this task I was appointed herald, envoy, and teacher; [12]that
is also why I must endure these difficulties, but they bring no
shame, for I know the one in whom I have lodged my trust and have
no doubt that he can preserve what has been entrusted to me until
that day. [13]Attend to the standard of sound instruction in the affec-
tionate trust of the Anointed Jesus, which you have learned from
me. [14]By the power of the holy spirit who dwells in us, maintain this
splendid benefit.

[15]As you know, all in Asia, including Phygelus and Hemogenes,
have abandoned me. [16]May the master have compassion upon the
Onesiphorus family, because he was a frequent source of strength
and took no offense at my incarceration. [17]On the contrary, no
sooner had he got to Rome than he set right out to look for and find
me. [18]May the master grant that he find compassion from the master on that day. You know at least as well as I how many services he
performed at Ephesus.

Paul's résumé.

- **1:12** Paul viewed hardships as apostolic qualifications, a view shared by popular philosophy, which stressed the difficulty of reaching the goals of a philosophical life.
- **1:12** *Entrusted* plays on the dominant theme of "guarding the deposit" (v. 14; 1 Tim 6:20).
- **1:13–14** The Pastor comes back to the point of v. 6, after providing evidence and edification. Reference to the spirit prevents a "bootstrap" theology. That spirit will keep Timothy on the true path.
- **1:15–18** Negative and positive examples follow. *All . . . have abandoned me* evokes pathos and the fate of Jesus. Hermogenes reappears in AcPaul 3, probably borrowed from 2 Timothy. There he is a blacksmith by trade. Onesiphorus represents the flip side. He is Paul's host in AcPaul 3–4. Reference to Rome implies that Paul engaged in more mission work after the incarceration reported in Acts 28 and that these labors, contrary to Romans 15, took place in the East. The entire scheme is probably fictional.
- **1:18** The first *master* probably refers to God, the second to Christ.

Timothy's Vocation

2 Σὺ οὖν, τέκνον μου, ἐνδυναμοῦ ἐν τῇ χάριτι τῇ ἐν Χριστῷ
Ἰησοῦ, 2καὶ ἃ ἤκουσας παρ' ἐμοῦ διὰ πολλῶν μαρτύρων, ταῦτα
παράθου πιστοῖς ἀνθρώποις, οἵτινες ἱκανοὶ ἔσονται καὶ ἑτέρους
διδάξαι. 3Συγκακοπάθησον ὡς καλὸς στρατιώτης Χριστοῦ Ἰησοῦ.
4οὐδεὶς στρατευόμενος ἐμπλέκεται ταῖς τοῦ βίου πραγματείαις, ἵνα
τῷ στρατολογήσαντι ἀρέσῃ. 5ἐὰν δὲ καὶ ἀθλῇ τις, οὐ στεφανοῦται
ἐὰν μὴ νομίμως ἀθλήσῃ. 6τὸν κοπιῶντα γεωργὸν δεῖ πρῶτον τῶν
καρπῶν μεταλαμβάνειν. 7νόει ὃ λέγω· δώσει γάρ σοι ὁ κύριος
σύνεσιν ἐν πᾶσιν.

Suffering

8Μνημόνευε Ἰησοῦν Χριστὸν ἐγηγερμένον ἐκ νεκρῶν, ἐκ
σπέρματος Δαυίδ, κατὰ τὸ εὐαγγέλιόν μου, 9ἐν ᾧ κακοπαθῶ μέχρι
δεσμῶν ὡς κακοῦργος, ἀλλ' ὁ λόγος τοῦ θεοῦ οὐ δέδεται· 10διὰ τοῦτο
πάντα ὑπομένω διὰ τοὺς ἐκλεκτούς, ἵνα καὶ αὐτοὶ σωτηρίας τύχωσιν
τῆς ἐν Χριστῷ Ἰησοῦ μετὰ δόξης αἰωνίου. 11πιστὸς ὁ λόγος·

εἰ γὰρ συναπεθάνομεν, καὶ συζήσομεν·
12εἰ ὑπομένομεν, καὶ συμβασιλεύσομεν·
εἰ ἀρνησόμεθα, κἀκεῖνος ἀρνήσεται ἡμᾶς·
13εἰ ἀπιστοῦμεν, ἐκεῖνος πιστὸς μένει,
ἀρνήσασθαι γὰρ ἑαυτὸν οὐ δύναται.

- **2:1–7** reiterate and develop earlier themes.
- **2:1–3** Grace is power, v. 2. Timothy's task is to pass on the tradition, v. 3: He will suffer, like Paul and Jesus before him. This is one element of the military imagery; cf. 1 Tim 1:18. The Pastor will elaborate these summary expressions with images.
- **2:2** *In the presence of* . . . is a desperate expedient. The normal meaning, "through," implies a slip: The actual audience is at the end of a chain of witnesses, beginning with Paul.
- **2:4–6** 1 Corinthians 9 probably inspired the trio of images from male life. Soldiers are to "settle their affairs" before active duty and keep their eyes on the task. Athletes keep their eyes on the prize and may not cheat, bend, or break rules. Farmers constitute a familiar trope for missionary labor. Cf. 1 Tim 5:18; Luke 17:7–10.
- **2:7** urges "Timothy" not just to repeat slogans but to think about them, and to trust Christ as a source of wisdom, i.e. to reflect Christologically.
- **2:8–15** develop Paul and Christ as examples. They are not on the same plane. Christ's victory empowers believers.

Timothy's Vocation

2 Therefore, my child, be strong because of what the Anointed Jesus gives. [2]Pass on what you have heard from me in the presence of many witnesses to trustworthy people, who thus will be competent to teach others. [3]As a good soldier of the Anointed Jesus, accept your share of hardships. [4]To please those who recruited them, enlistees avoid entanglement in civilian concerns. [5]Competing athletes cannot gain the prize if they don't play by the rules. [6]Hardworking farmers are first to receive a share of the harvest. [7]Consider what I am telling you: the master will provide you with insight into everything.

Suffering

[8]Be mindful of Jesus Christ, raised from the dead, descended from David. That's my message. [9]Because of it I have to put up with being jailed like a common criminal. God's word, however, has not been locked up, [10]and so I put up with everything for the sake of the chosen, so that they might experience deliverance by the Anointed Jesus, as well as endless splendor. [11]This is the gospel truth:

> For if we died with him we shall also live with him.
> [12]If we endure, we shall also reign with him.
> If we deny, Christ will deny us
> [13]If we do not keep the faith, Christ remains trustworthy,
> for he cannot deny himself.

- **2:8** reverses the order of Rom 1:3–4. The Pastor chooses not to write in salvation-historical order. Resurrection is primary. Davidic descent is less a messianic claim than an affirmation of Jesus' humanity. Unlike Luke, for example, the Pastor views Christ's resurrection in terms of its meaning for believers rather than as the revival of a corpse. Paul, likewise, does not view his suffering as the price of a ticket to heaven but as suffering for others. This is not self-centered; it also presents the apostle as a Christ figure whose suffering frees others.
- **2:11–13** Here the *gospel truth* saying points forward to the creedal hymn, made up of four conditional sentences. The first two mark the apodosis (result clause) with *also*. The second pair uses an emphatic pronoun, rendered *Christ* here. The same pronoun (*ekeinos*) is used for the "Paraclete" in John 16 and Christ in 1 John 2. Verse 12b reflects the saying found in Luke 12:9. Pol-Phil 2:5 is quite similar, although not evidently dependent upon 2 Timothy. The final line may well be the Pastor's addition. The hymn is a baptismal confession, like Rom 6:3–11. The presupposition is that the redeemed share the fate of the redeemer.

Rival Teaching

14Ταῦτα ὑπομίμνησκε διαμαρτυρόμενος ἐνώπιον τοῦ θεοῦ μὴ
λογομαχεῖν, ἐπ' οὐδὲν χρήσιμον, ἐπὶ καταστροφῇ τῶν ἀκουόντων.
15σπούδασον σεαυτὸν δόκιμον παραστῆσαι τῷ θεῷ, ἐργάτην
ἀνεπαίσχυντον, ὀρθοτομοῦντα τὸν λόγον τῆς ἀληθείας. 16τὰς δὲ
βεβήλους κενοφωνίας περιΐστασο· ἐπὶ πλεῖον γὰρ προκόψουσιν
ἀσεβείας. 17καὶ ὁ λόγος αὐτῶν ὡς γάγγραινα νομὴν ἕξει. ὧν ἐστιν
Ὑμέναιος καὶ Φίλητος, 18οἵτινες περὶ τὴν ἀλήθειαν ἠστόχησαν,
λέγοντες [τὴν] ἀνάστασιν ἤδη γεγονέναι, καὶ ἀνατρέπουσιν τήν
τινων πίστιν. 19ὁ μέντοι στερεὸς θεμέλιος τοῦ θεοῦ ἕστηκεν, ἔχων
τὴν σφραγῖδα ταύτην· ἔγνω κύριος τοὺς ὄντας αὐτοῦ, καί· ἀποστήτω
ἀπὸ ἀδικίας πᾶς ὁ ὀνομάζων τὸ ὄνομα κυρίου. 20Ἐν μεγάλῃ δὲ
οἰκίᾳ οὐκ ἔστιν μόνον σκεύη χρυσᾶ καὶ ἀργυρᾶ ἀλλὰ καὶ ξύλινα
καὶ ὀστράκινα, καὶ ἃ μὲν εἰς τιμὴν ἃ δὲ εἰς ἀτιμίαν· 21ἐὰν οὖν τις
ἐκκαθάρῃ ἑαυτὸν ἀπὸ τούτων, ἔσται σκεῦος εἰς τιμήν, ἡγιασμένον,
εὔχρηστον τῷ δεσπότῃ, εἰς πᾶν ἔργον ἀγαθὸν ἡτοιμασμένον.

22Τὰς δὲ νεωτερικὰς ἐπιθυμίας φεῦγε, δίωκε δὲ δικαιοσύνην
πίστιν ἀγάπην εἰρήνην μετὰ τῶν ἐπικαλουμένων τὸν κύριον ἐκ
καθαρᾶς καρδίας. 23τὰς δὲ μωρὰς καὶ ἀπαιδεύτους ζητήσεις παραιτοῦ,

---

2:14 Choices are "God" or "the Lord." The latter could be Christ. For "God" see 1 Tim 5:4, 21; 2 Tim 4:1.
2:18 The article in *the resurrection* may not be original, but the translation probably requires it.

- **2:14–26** The dismal and redundant theme reappears: The best way to deal with rival messages is avoidance of debate.
- **2:16** *Mundane jargon* is the approximate opposite of godly expression. Since correct doctrine yields good behavior—coherence of words and deeds—the opponents must, of necessity, be moral failures. We don't talk to our opponents, but we can caricature their views.
- **2:17** Note the medical imagery, derived from popular philosophy. Our views are wholesome. Theirs will rot the whole barrel. See "Sound Teaching," p. 33.
- **2:17–18** *Hymenaeus.* Cf. 1 Tim 5:20; this is the sole mention of *Philetus.* The author actually cites a doctrinal postulate of the opposition: [The] resurrection has occurred. This refers to believers. One can associate this with behavioral elements to construct a profile. See the Introduction under "Rival Teaching." AcPaul 3:14 assigns this view to Demas and Hermogenes. Not often do the Pastor and the author of the Acts of Paul find themselves on the same page.
- **2:18** *Wrecking* prepares for the subsequent building (house) imagery.
- **2:19** Foundation imagery (derived from Isa 28:16) is widespread: Mark 12:10; 1 Cor 3:31; Eph 2:20 are examples. For the Pastor the foundation is not Christ

Rival Teaching

[14]Keep this message before their eyes while strongly declaring, as God is your witness, that they avoid mere disputes about terms, which is good for nothing and may ruin the participants. [15]Eagerly present yourself to God as reliable, a worker with no regrets, properly teaching the genuine message. [16]Shun mundane jargon. Those who use it progress from impiety to impiety. [17]Their message will grow like gangrene. Examples of such growth are Hymenaeus and Philetus, [18]who strayed from the true path by announcing "The resurrection has already happened," wrecking some people's belief. [19]Nonetheless God's firm foundation stands fast, inscribed with these words: "The master knows his own," and "Let all who appeal to the master's name avoid wrongdoing." [20]Grand houses possess not only gold and silver vessels, but also some of wood and clay. The former hold places of honor; the latter serve baser ends. [21]Those who purge themselves of the base will become honorable vessels, consecrated, useful to the head of the household, ready for every good activity.

[22]Flee youthful passions and strive after justice, trust, affection, and good relations with all who appeal to the master from pure hearts. [23]Stay away from stupid and uninformed speculations. You

---

but sound doctrine. The foundation is protected by a seal, which in this case is two inscribed phrases. They are not citations, although evidently inspired by Num 16:25 and Isa 26:13. The Pastor's attitude toward the OT is remarkable.

- **2:20–21** The metaphor shifts from house to contents. The imagery does not seem consistent. Homes may have sterling and good china as well as garbage pails and boxes for cat litter. One does not serve Sunday dinner in the latter. Honorable and dishonorable represent sound and false teachers. The community is a mixed body. Verse 21 says that these utensils can be cleaned, that is, that bad teachers could repent. If the Pastor is talking about transformation, fashioning clay into gold, the image might hold. (This imagery flourished in deterministic circles. Dualists spoke of wisdom/soul as a drop of gold in the mud or a pearl in a worthless shell. Is the Pastor borrowing a leaf from the opponents' book?)
- **2:22–26** The text moves from personal advice to general statements. *Youthful passions* are probably rage rather than sexual lust. Verses 24–26 give a silver plate, if not a gold wash, to the entire unit. Christians would rather win people than arguments. Knockout punches quiet opponents but do not change their minds. The Pastor knows that honey catches more flies than does vinegar.

εἰδὼς ὅτι γεννῶσιν μάχας· [24]δοῦλον δὲ κυρίου οὐ δεῖ μάχεσθαι ἀλλ'
ἤπιον εἶναι πρὸς πάντας, διδακτικόν, ἀνεξίκακον, [25]ἐν πραΰτητι
παιδεύοντα τοὺς ἀντιδιατιθεμένους, μήποτε δώῃ αὐτοῖς ὁ θεὸς
μετάνοιαν εἰς ἐπίγνωσιν ἀληθείας [26]καὶ ἀνανήψωσιν ἐκ τῆς τοῦ
διαβόλου παγίδος, ἐζωγρημένοι ὑπ' αὐτοῦ εἰς τὸ ἐκείνου θέλημα.

3 Τοῦτο δὲ γίνωσκε, ὅτι ἐν ἐσχάταις ἡμέραις ἐνστήσονται καιροὶ
χαλεποί [2]ἔσονται γὰρ οἱ ἄνθρωποι φίλαυτοι φιλάργυροι ἀλαζόνες
ὑπερήφανοι βλάσφημοι, γονεῦσιν ἀπειθεῖς, ἀχάριστοι ἀνόσιοι
[3]ἄστοργοι ἄσπονδοι διάβολοι ἀκρατεῖς ἀνήμεροι ἀφιλάγαθοι
[4]προδόται προπετεῖς ετυφωμένοι, φιλήδονοι μᾶλλον ἢ φιλόθεοι,
[5]ἔχοντες μόρφωσιν εὐσεβείας τὴν δὲ δύναμιν αὐτῆς ἠρνημένοι·
καὶ τούτους ἀποτρέπου. [6]ἐκ τούτων γάρ εἰσιν οἱ ἐνδύνοντες εἰς τὰς
οἰκίας καὶ αἰχμαλωτίζοντες γυναικάρια σεσωρευμένα ἁμαρτίαις,
ἀγόμενα ἐπιθυμίαις ποικίλαις, [7]πάντοτε μανθάνοντα καὶ μηδέποτε
εἰς ἐπίγνωσιν ἀληθείας ἐλθεῖν δυνάμενα. [8]ὃν τρόπον δὲ Ἰάννης
καὶ Ἰαμβρῆς ἀντέστησαν Μωϋσεῖ, οὕτως καὶ οὗτοι ἀνθίστανται τῇ
ἀληθείᾳ, ἄνθρωποι κατεφθαρμένοι τὸν νοῦν, ἀδόκιμοι περὶ τὴν
πίστιν. [9]ἀλλ' οὐ προκόψουσιν ἐπὶ πλεῖον· ἡ γὰρ ἄνοια αὐτῶν ἔκδηλος
ἔσται πᾶσιν, ὡς καὶ ἡ ἐκείνων ἐγένετο.

Paul's Suffering

[10]Σὺ δὲ παρηκολούθησάς μου τῇ διδασκαλίᾳ, τῇ ἀγωγῇ, τῇ
προθέσει, τῇ πίστει, τῇ μακροθυμίᾳ, τῇ ἀγάπῃ, τῇ ὑπομονῇ, [11]τοῖς
διωγμοῖς, τοῖς παθήμασιν, οἷά μοι ἐγένετο ἐν Ἀντιοχείᾳ, ἐν Ἰκονίῳ,
ἐν Λύστροις, οἵους διωγμοὺς ὑπήνεγκα καὶ ἐκ πάντων με ἐρρύσατο

3:11 Between *Antioch* and *Iconium* ms 181 (eleventh century) and the Harclean Syriac (sixth century or later) insert "that is what he suffered on account of Thecla; and what believers in Christ experienced from the Jews." This appears to be a gloss (a marginal note, such as are still made in books), as indicated by the shift from *I* to *he* and the implied *they* of the second clause. Confirmation comes from the ninth century codex (book) K, where it is found in the margin. The glossator has combined two sources, viewed as of equal historical value: AcPaul 4 and Acts 14. The practice of filling in gaps and details in the epistles from Acts continues in the present.

- **3:1–9** focus upon the opposition, its implicit cause, and its successes. Verses 10–17 treat means of combatting them, with assurances.
- **3:1** Cf. 1 Tim 4:1. Last days give wickedness its last chance. These two passages are variations upon the theme of false teaching and its suppression.
- **3:2–5** illustrates the above with a list of nearly twenty bad qualities, jingly and often alliterative, ending with advice to avoid such types. Their words contrast to their deeds.

know that they generate quarrels. 24Christ's slaves must not get into quarrels, but rather be gentle toward all, good teachers, and hard to upset, 25as they correct opponents politely. God just might lead them to change their minds and grasp knowledge of the truth, 26that is, come to their senses, and, taken over by God to serve the divine will, elude the devil's traps.

3 Know this: in the final days dreadful times will arrive. 2There will be no lack of those who are selfish, avaricious, boastful, arrogant, denigrating, disrespectful to their parents, ungrateful, unholy, 3loveless, irreconcilable, scurrilous, dissolute, brutal, inimical to good, 4treacherous, reckless, conceited, more fond of pleasure than of God, 5manifesting the trappings of the spiritual life while denying its capability. Avoid such people. 6Some of this ilk will insinuate themselves into households and beguile stupid women inundated with sins, susceptible to every kind of craving, 7ever "learning" but never able to achieve genuine knowledge. 8These people oppose truth as Jannes and Jambres opposed Moses. They are mental degenerates, unqualified in matters of the faith. 9They have reached the end of their road, for their folly is no less evident to everyone than was that of the two magicians just named.

Paul's Suffering

10You, however, adhered to my teaching, way of life, consistency, belief, patience, affection, endurance, 11persecutions, and sufferings. The sufferings experienced in Pisidian Antioch, Iconium, and Lystra! The persecutions I endured there! But the master delivered

---

- **3:6** The rivals' tactics are house-based. From one angle they are exploiting the vulnerable. Cf. Origen, *Cels.* 3.55. For a different approach, imagine that they urge women to overcome their vulnerability and its causes. The Pastor once more invokes the misogynist stereotype that women are readily seducible. Cf. 1 Tim 2:8–15.
- **3:7** concedes the intellectual interest of the rivals.
- **3:8–9** Just as the author often mentions pairs of opponents, such as Phygelus and Hermogenes (1 Tim 1:15), so a historical pair of famous magicians serve as negative examples. The Pastor rarely cites known biblical passages, but he presumes that the (now lost) apocryphal biography of Jannes and Jambres is generally familiar—at least to the implied addressee. The duo's activities ranged from serving Pharaoh as court sorcerers to promoting the cult of the Golden Calf. Despite such typological antecedents, the opposition has made inroads (3:9), but their day is over.
- **3:10–13** Paul is a living catalogue of virtues, which Timothy has followed. Verse 11 is based upon Acts 13–14. What happened to Paul will happen to all.

ὁ κύριος. 12καὶ πάντες δὲ οἱ θέλοντες εὐσεβῶς ζῆν ἐν Χριστῷ Ἰησοῦ
διωχθήσονται. 13πονηροὶ δὲ ἄνθρωποι καὶ γόητες προκόψουσιν ἐπὶ
τὸ χεῖρον πλανῶντες καὶ πλανώμενοι.

Timothy's Vocation

14Σὺ δὲ μένε ἐν οἷς ἔμαθες καὶ ἐπιστώθης, εἰδὼς παρὰ τίνων
ἔμαθες, 15καὶ ὅτι ἀπὸ βρέφους [τὰ] ἱερὰ γράμματα οἶδας, τὰ δυνάμενά
σε σοφίσαι εἰς σωτηρίαν διὰ πίστεως τῆς ἐν Χριστῷ Ἰησοῦ. 16πᾶσα
γραφὴ θεόπνευστος καὶ ὠφέλιμος πρὸς διδασκαλίαν, πρὸς ἐλεγμόν,
πρὸς ἐπανόρθωσιν, πρὸς παιδείαν τὴν ἐν δικαιοσύνῃ, 17ἵνα ἄρτιος ᾖ
ὁ τοῦ θεοῦ ἄνθρωπος, πρὸς πᾶν ἔργον ἀγαθὸν ἐξηρτισμένος.

4 Διαμαρτύρομαι ἐνώπιον τοῦ θεοῦ καὶ Χριστοῦ Ἰησοῦ τοῦ
μέλλοντος κρίνειν ζῶντας καὶ νεκρούς, καὶ τὴν ἐπιφάνειαν αὐτοῦ

3:14 In place of the plural *whom* a range of witnesses read the singular, effectively making Paul Timothy's sole teacher.
4:1 The awkward *and the arrival of* . . . is improved in many witnesses by replacing "and" with a preposition showing the means of judgment (replacing *kai* with *kata*). This illustrates the text-critical principle of *lectio difficilior*: more difficult readings are often preferable, since editors and scribes are less likely to make an intelligible text obscure than vice-versa.

- **3:14–17** include a brief encomium of another resource: scripture. Of its merits the Pastor is not, as just noted, a good example, but he has provided proponents of "biblical Christianity" with a favorite proof for their claims. The translation of v. 16 is uncertain. "All scripture is inspired" is possible, but quite trite. The syntax suggests "every inspired (and useful) writing." "Every scripture is inspired and useful" is slightly less preferable. Verse 15 spoke of "sacred writings" (*hiera grammata*). The term "writing" (*graphē*) has

Scripture

The term *graphē*, often rendered "scripture," had a broader sense in the early Christian era. Although the meaning in 2 Tim 3:15–16 (which also employs a similar word, *grammata)* approximates something like "the Bible" (that is, the LXX, the Greek version of the OT) used by early Christians, one should not assume that the word carries all of the freight it bore in the fourth and later centuries. "Authoritative text" or "writing" is an adequate if cumbersome translation. One should also bear in mind that the number of books in the LXX varied considerably

me from all of them. [12]Persecution will befall all who attempt the pious life oriented to the Anointed Jesus. [13]The wicked and fraudulent
will go from bad to worse, deceived deceivers.

Timothy's Vocation

[14]For your part stick with what you have learned and found convincing, since you know from whom your learning came. [15]Since
childhood you have come to know the sacred writings, which can
give you the wisdom leading to deliverance through trust in the
Anointed Jesus. [16]Every bit of scripture imbued by God is also profitable for teaching, for criticism, for edification, for teaching what is
right, [17]so that the godly might be equipped and proficient for every
fine deed.

4 I adjure you, in the sight of God and the Anointed Jesus, who
will come to judge living and dead, and the arrival of his dominion:

---

a broader application. The closing verses describe its utility in the tool chest of the godly. Usefulness rather than inspiration receives the emphasis. The Pastor does not here accuse the rivals of misusing biblical texts. The stress in v. 16 is upon moral guidelines rather than sacred history, whereas v. 15 could be applied to "biblical prophecies" or other Christological applications.

- **2 Timothy 4** is memorable for its crisp, pithy short phrases, often with asyndeton (no connective words), many of which are familiar English phrases (via the version of 1611).
- **4:1–6** is the final exhortation. Impending death provided a suitable setting for eschatological discussion. The Pastor is mindful of the difficulties that will come after Paul's departure. Cf. Acts 20:29–31.

and that few communities had complete collections of these sacred writings.

Inspiration was not the highest honor that could be assigned to a text. Until at least 200 CE inspiration was a quality enjoyed by many believers and their literary products.

Only at 1 Tim 5:18 does the author cite *graphē*. The texts quoted are 1 Cor 9:9 and Luke 10:7. This does not mean that the Pastor viewed Luke and Paul as parts of the Bible, although it does show that these writings were authoritative for him.

καὶ τὴν βασιλείαν αὐτοῦ· 2κήρυξον τὸν λόγον, ἐπίστηθι εὐκαίρως
ἀκαίρως, ἔλεγξον, ἐπιτίμησον, παρακάλεσον, ἐν πάσῃ μακροθυμίᾳ
καὶ διδαχῇ. 3Ἔσται γὰρ καιρὸς ὅτε τῆς ὑγιαινούσης διδασκαλίας οὐκ
ἀνέξονται ἀλλὰ κατὰ τὰς ἰδίας ἐπιθυμίας ἑαυτοῖς ἐπισωρεύσουσιν
διδασκάλους κνηθόμενοι τὴν ἀκοὴν 4καὶ ἀπὸ μὲν τῆς ἀληθείας τὴν
ἀκοὴν ἀποστρέψουσιν, ἐπὶ δὲ τοὺς μύθους ἐκτραπήσονται. 5Σὺ δὲ
νῆφε ἐν πᾶσιν, κακοπάθησον, ἔργον ποίησον εὐαγγελιστοῦ, τὴν
διακονίαν σου πληροφόρησον.

Peroration

6Ἐγὼ γὰρ ἤδη σπένδομαι, καὶ ὁ καιρὸς τῆς ἀναλύσεώς μου
ἐφέστηκεν. 7τὸν καλὸν ἀγῶνα ἠγώνισμαι, τὸν δρόμον τετέλεκα, τὴν
πίστιν τετήρηκα· 8λοιπὸν ἀπόκειταί μοι ὁ τῆς δικαιοσύνης στέφανος,
ὃν ἀποδώσει μοι ὁ κύριος ἐν ἐκείνῃ τῇ ἡμέρᾳ, ὁ δίκαιος κριτής, οὐ
μόνον δὲ ἐμοὶ ἀλλὰ καὶ πᾶσι τοῖς ἠγαπηκόσι τὴν ἐπιφάνειαν αὐτοῦ.
9Σπούδασον ἐλθεῖν πρός με ταχέως· 10Δημᾶς γάρ με ἐγκατέλιπεν
ἀγαπήσας τὸν νῦν αἰῶνα καὶ ἐπορεύθη εἰς Θεσσαλονίκην, Κρήσκης
εἰς Γαλατίαν, Τίτος εἰς Δαλματίαν· 11Λουκᾶς ἐστιν μόνος μετ᾽ ἐμοῦ.
Μᾶρκον ἀναλαβὼν ἄγε μετὰ σεαυτοῦ, ἔστιν γάρ μοι εὔχρηστος εἰς

4:2 Alexandrinus (see under Titus 1:9) adds, from 2:3, "as a good soldier of the Anointed Jesus," after *put up with evil.* This illustrates the tendency to enrich and expand texts by phrases from other texts.
4:10 A variety of witnesses read "Gaul" instead of *Galatia.* What is now France could be called "Galatia" in antiquity. Referring the word to "Gaul" would expand the horizon of the Pauline mission, a project that would be welcomed by believers living in that western province. The same problem appears in the text of AcPaul 14:1.

- **4:2** Jesus serves as judge only in Deuteropauline writings, e.g., 2 Thess 2:12 (within the Pauline tradition).
- **4:2** *Convenient.* This intimates that Timothy is to take the gloves off, but the "Give 'em hell, Harry" recommendation is tempered by reference to patient instruction.
- **4:4** *False stories.* Cf. 1 Tim 1:4 and Titus 1:14. The small corpus is effectively bracketed by reference to the appeal of narrative as utilized by the rivals.
- **4:5** summarizes the work of ministry, enumerating categories that may be filled in as needed.
- **4:6–7** The images cohere in sequence. Athletic contests were religious festivals, which would open with a sacrificial libation. Few could afford an ox, but nearly everyone could spill a few drops in recognition that all things came from God/the gods. Paul is that libation. Three ringing declarations follow. Sporting metaphors were useful because they viewed life as a struggle requiring training and discipline. (On athletic imagery see 1 Tim 4:7; 6:12.). "Run the race." See Acts 20:24 (and 13:25). "Keeping faith" has its

[2]proclaim the message; be ready when it is convenient and when
it is not. Correct, chastise, encourage, with perfect patience and
whatever instruction is required. [3]The time will come when people
won't tolerate wholesome teaching, but will collect droves of teachers who will tickle their ears and pander to their desires. [4]They will
turn those ears from the truth to false stories. [5]You, on the contrary,
must always be prudent, put up with evil, proclaim the great message, and neglect no part of your service.

Peroration

[6]For I am already being sacrificed; the time of my departure has
arrived. [7]I have completed the noble contest; I have run the race; I
have kept the faith. [8]The next step will be the well-deserved crown
reserved for me. The Master, the fair judge will award it on that
day—and not only to me but to all who long for his arrival.

[9]Do your utmost to come to me promptly, for [10]Demas, in his
fondness for this life, has abandoned me and gone to Thessalonica.
Crescens went to Galatia; Titus to Dalmatia. [11]Luke alone has remained by my side. Get Mark and bring him with you. He can be a

---

obvious religious significance; it also fits into the general metaphor, for athletes had to mind the rules, sometimes giving pledge under oath. Crowns go to victors. Paul, in fact, looked like a loser. (Winners in the major games got to enjoy something like ease in Zion, for most never had to work again.)

- **4:9–22** Paul forgets everything that he has written hitherto. Although on the verge of death, he showers Timothy with requests, not all short-range in nature. About this claim one may seek to quibble, for vv. 9–18 run the "apostolic parousia" theme in reverse: Paul summons colleagues to his side so that he need not die lonely and abandoned, although he will milk that possibility for all that it is worth. What is less comprehensible or excusable is that, after nine plus chapters of instruction and advice, he orders Timothy to drop everything and hasten to his side. This is to say that the various personalia and other details are among the least probable and most fictional elements in the PE.
- **4:10–15** The author is mainly dependent upon the greetings list in Philemon 24, expanded in Col 4:10. *Demas'* fondness for this life is developed in the AcPaul 3. *Crescens* is original to the PE (a person with the same Latin name carries Polycarp's letter, PolPhil 14). Titus, evidently at Rome (!), has left. In the AcPaul 14 Titus returns from Dalmatia and Luke from Gaul/Galatia. If *Mark* always refers to the same person, he came from Jerusalem (Acts 12) and, after association with Paul, was with Peter in Rome (1 Pet 5:13). *Tychicus* is linked to Ephesus (Acts 20:4) and appears in Col 4:7, Eph 6:21, and Titus 3:12.

διακονίαν. [12]Τύχικον δὲ ἀπέστειλα εἰς Ἔφεσον. [13]τὸν φαιλόνην ὃν
ἀπέλιπον ἐν Τρῳάδι παρὰ Κάρπῳ ἐρχόμενος φέρε, καὶ τὰ βιβλία
μάλιστα τὰς μεμβράνας. [14]Ἀλέξανδρος ὁ χαλκεὺς πολλά μοι κακὰ
ἐνεδείξατο· ἀποδώσει αὐτῷ ὁ κύριος κατὰ τὰ ἔργα αὐτοῦ· [15]ὃν καὶ σὺ
φυλάσσου, λίαν γὰρ ἀντέστη τοῖς ἡμετέροις λόγοις.

[16]Ἐν τῇ πρώτῃ μου ἀπολογίᾳ οὐδείς μοι παρεγένετο, ἀλλὰ πάντες
με ἐγκατέλιπον· μὴ αὐτοῖς λογισθείη [17]ὁ δὲ κύριός μοι παρέστη
καὶ ἐνεδυνάμωσέν με, ἵνα δι᾽ ἐμοῦ τὸ κήρυγμα πληροφορηθῇ καὶ
ἀκούσωσιν πάντα τὰ ἔθνη, καὶ ἐρρύσθην ἐκ στόματος λέοντος.
[18]ῥύσεταί με ὁ κύριος ἀπὸ παντὸς ἔργου πονηροῦ καὶ σώσει εἰς τὴν
βασιλείαν αὐτοῦ τὴν ἐπουράνιον·

ᾧ ἡ δόξα εἰς τοὺς αἰῶνας τῶν αἰώνων, ἀμήν.

Epistolary Close

[19]Ἄσπασαι Πρίσκαν καὶ Ἀκύλαν καὶ τὸν Ὀνησιφόρου οἶκον.
[20]Ἔραστος ἔμεινεν ἐν Κορίνθῳ, Τρόφιμον δὲ ἀπέλιπον ἐν Μιλήτῳ
ἀσθενοῦντα. [21]Σπούδασον πρὸ χειμῶνος ἐλθεῖν. Ἀσπάζεταί σε
Εὔβουλος καὶ Πούδης καὶ Λίνος καὶ Κλαυδία καὶ οἱ ἀδελφοὶ πάντες.

[22]Ὁ κύριος μετὰ τοῦ πνεύματός σου. ἡ χάρις μεθ᾽ ὑμῶν.

4:19 Ms 181 (see under 3:11, above) and 460 (thirteenth century) insert, awkwardly, in modification of *Onesiphorus' family*, "Lectra, his wife, and his sons Simmias and Zeno." The source is AcPaul 2:2.
4:22 *Master* is expanded in several witnesses. "With us" is an unlikely variant. Several D-Texts supply a different closing: "Farewell in peace." Its origin is difficult to explain, and it may therefore be original.

As usual, closing notes appear in the fourth century and become increasingly elaborate over time.

- **4:13** Paul has not a coat on his back. In addition he would like some material for reading and writing. *Carpus* is otherwise unknown.
- **4:14** See 1 Tim 1:20. The opposition of metalworkers in Acts 19 has long legs, stretching from Acts 19 to the PE to the Acts of Paul.

real help to me. [12]I sent Tychicus back to Ephesus. [13]When you come,
pick up the cloak I left at Troas with Carpus, as well as the scrolls,
and especially, the notebooks. [14]Alexander the coppersmith has
done me much harm. The master will give him what he has earned.
[15]You, too, be on the alert for him, because he has vigorously opposed what I say.

[16]At my first hearing no one came to help. In fact, they all deserted me. I hope that God does not hold this against them. [17]Still,
the master stood by and supported me, so that the message might
be disseminated by me and all the gentiles hear it. So I was delivered from the jaws of a lion. [18]The master will deliver me from every
wicked action and preserve me for his transcendent dominion.

To Christ be splendor for ever and ever. Amen

Epistolary Close

[19]Greet Prisca, Aquila, and the Onesiphorus family. [20]Erastus
stayed in Corinth. I left Trophimus in Miletus because he was ill.
[21]Please get here before winter. Greetings from Eubulus, Pudens,
Linus, Claudia, and all the believers.

[22]The master be with you in spirit. Grace be with all of you.

- **4:16** *First hearing* is ambiguous. That it refers to an early acquittal years earlier is not very likely. Pathos reappears.
- **4:17** *Jaws of a lion* is a common metaphor. On the basis of 1 Cor 15:32 the Acts of Paul transform the trope into a literal, yet charming, story.
- **4:19** *Prisca* and *Aquila* are back in Ephesus (1 Cor 16:19; AcPaul 9). On *the Onesiphorus family* see 1:16.
- **4:20** An *Erastus* appears with Timothy at Acts 19:22; here Rom 16:20 is evoked. *Trophimus* was part of the collection delegation in Acts 20–21.
- **4:21** Since travel was avoided in winter, this reinforces the need for haste. Nothing is known of the four named here, although Irenaeus, *Haer.* 3.3.3, states that *Linus* became bishop of Rome.
- **4:22** is a typical Pauline close.

POLYCARP

INTRODUCTION

1. Polycarp, Smyrna, Philippi

Smyrna, an ancient city on the west coast of Asia Minor (and reputed hometown of Homer), prospered throughout the Roman period and was notable for architecture as well as medical and scientific studies. The city was a center of the rhetorical movement known as the Second Sophistic, a leading representative of which, Aelius Aristides, resided there.[1] Dying a good generation earlier than Aristides was the bishop of Smyrna's Christian community, Polycarp. If Polycarp gives interviews in heaven, he will be in considerable demand, for his life stretched from the last lingering foothills of the apostolic era into the heyday of the Apologists (c. 70–75 to c. 155–60 CE). Irenaeus, bishop of Lyons (c. 180), according to a letter cited by Eusebius (*Hist. eccl.* 5.20.4–8), claims that, as a young boy, he heard Polycarp's reminiscences about the apostle John. This is highly unlikely, for he shows no knowledge of the gospel attributed to John, but it does reveal Polycarp's place in early Christian imagination.

Polycarp was the recipient of a letter from Ignatius (if genuine), the author of correspondence with Philippi (PolPhil), and the subject of a moving and model martyrdom story.[2] Four points in his career stand out: Interaction with Ignatius, that correspondence with the Philippians, a visit to Rome and its bishop Anicetus (c. 155–c. 166), and his martyrdom. For Irenaeus he was not only a great link in the chain of tradition, but a stout warrior for what the bishop of Lyons viewed as correct belief.

One does not see that judgment reflected in his Philippians. The great student of ancient prose rhythm, Eduard Norden, observed:

> In the strongest imaginable contrast to Ignatius' letters stands the letter of one who befriended him, Polycarp of Smyrna (d. 155 or 156) to the Philippians. . . . One reads him quickly without disruption, while Ignatius

1. See the survey of Potter, "Smyrna." On its history see Cadoux, *Ancient Smyrna*. Akurgal, *Ancient Civilizations*, 119–24, surveys the material remains.

2. A biography of Polycarp attributed to one Pionius is of no detectable historical value.

> presents problems in nearly every sentence. One cannot either praise or criticize his language, there is no unfamiliar expression, no anacoluthon, but also no original idea, no rhetoric of either heart or head (e.g., no antithesis). The only thing he has in common with his friend is a martyr's death.[3]

If elegant rhetoric was part of the atmosphere of Smyrna, Polycarp must have lived on imported bottled oxygen. Those who turn to this author for the first time are likely to sense also a convincing lack of originality. These reactions do not comprise the entire story. Polycarp may appear artless, but he builds his argument with such skill that readers do not find themselves moved until the point has been made. More importantly, Polycarp has a fine pastoral sense. Although an ardent exponent of the ethical life, he never loses sight of the danger posed to Christian community by the judgmental wrath of the self-appointed guardians of righteousness. Enticing style and scintillating content are not everything. The Pastor is always talking about wholesome fare. Polycarp simply provides it.

His correspondents were believers at Philippi, a Pauline foundation (11:3). The Macedonian churches were for Paul a source of apostolic pride (2 Cor 8:1). Philippi was a strategic site, on a pass between two hills. An earlier city was enlarged by Philip II of Macedon in 356. This required a new name. After due meditation and consultation the king hit upon "Philippi," and so it remained. There Caesar's heirs crushed the opposition, and the city became a Roman colony, a piece of the mother city. The Aegean united those on either side of the water. Although Acts 16 is not readily reconciled with the Pauline correspondence, the account highlights the importance of Paul's gentile mission in the region. After the passage of Ignatius and the correspondence of Polycarp, silence falls upon this church.[4]

2. The Text

Fate was less kind than Eduard Norden to Polycarp's correspondence. All of the Greek manuscripts, stemming from the eleventh to the thirteenth centuries, leap from the middle of PolPhil 9:2 to Barn 5:7. The lost archetype was an edition of the Apostolic Fathers that was missing some leaves. If

3. *Die antike Kunstprosa*, vol. 2, 512 (author's trans.).

4. Until Dionysius of Corinth (c. 170) almost nothing of value is known from the Christian history of the west side of the Aegean, whereas information about Asia Minor is relatively plentiful. On the colony see Koukouli-Chrysantaki, "Colonia Iulia Augusta Philippensis." In-depth studies include Bormann, *Philippi*, and Pilhofer, *Philippi*, vol. 1. Hendrix, "Philippi," has a good brief survey.

the first copyist noted a gap, subsequent scribes failed to report it. In his *Ecclesiastical History* 3.36.13–15, Eusebius preserved chapter 9 (without the last sentence) and chapter 13 in Greek, the earliest evidence for Polycarp's text. For the residue scholars must resort to a Latin translation, based upon a better Greek text than our manuscripts, but the merits of this version are disputed. If they must depend upon a translation, scholars prefer that it be painfully literal and unimaginative.

3. Genre and Structure

PolPhil is a conventional early Christian letter, the form of which follows 1 Clement (written c. 95). It is a letter of moral advice, a type with links to the popular philosophical tradition.[5] Included genres are the Church Order (the earliest extant independent example of which is the *Didachē*) and the Household Code, Christian forms of which appear imbedded within letters from Colossians onward. (See the Introduction to the PE.) Generically, PolPhil is at home in the outer periphery of the Deuteropauline world, with close links to 1 Timothy and Titus (on which see below). Polycarp may have acquired his literary content and means from early Christian texts—which is not a claim that he lacked education but that his generation laid the groundwork of a Christian culture.

The structure is uncomplicated, perhaps deceptively so.

4. Occasion and Circumstances

The known interaction between the Christian communities at Smyrna and Philippi was a result of the martyrdom of Ignatius (on the date of which see below), who passed through both cities en route to Rome for execution (the reasons for which are unknown). At some point believers at Philippi wrote to Smyrna; they also requested that Polycarp supply them with copies of Ignatius' correspondence in his possession (PolPhil 13). The Philippians also asked Polycarp to share with them his thoughts about "righteousness" (*dikaiosynē*). In Pauline discourse this word is often rendered "justification." For Polycarp—and others, probably including Philippians—it means "doing the right thing" and is translated "correct behavior." PolPhil reveals that one Valens, described as "a presbyter of yours" or "your presbyter," who may

5. For a good short discussion of these types and typical contents see Holmes, "Polycarp of Smyrna," 110–12.

have been the pastor,[6] had given up or been deprived of his office evidently because of financial irregularities. How do these data interrelate? Was all of the information conveyed in one letter and one response? Did the person or persons who conveyed the request for a treatise on righteousness supply the information about Valens orally? Did a link exist between the teaching attacked in PolPhil 7 and debates about righteousness or anything else at Philippi? Definitive answers are impossible. The most prudent approach is to interpret PolPhil as it stands while subordinating contextual hypotheses. This will distort the meaning, for letters are parts of a conversation, but it is preferable to interpreting the correspondence against a reconstructed and inevitably contentious background. One introductory question where debate continues to flourish is that of unity.

5. The Unity of Polycarp to the Philippians

The question is whether PolPhil represents a single letter or is an amalgam of two. At one time this matter was fundamental to dating the material, but now it is largely at exercise in and illustration of methodological issues. The cause of the change is a general tendency to date the death of Ignatius in the second half of Hadrian's reign, that is, 130–35 or even later.[7] This places Polycarp's correspondence in the fourth decade of the second century.[8]

A common, if not always explicit, assumption holds that documents should be presumed to stand in their original condition until proven otherwise beyond reasonable doubt. This would be valid if those responsible for transmitting early Christian letters had the worthy scholarly goals of preserving their original contexts, but they did not. Early proponents of the correspondence quite logically wished to present Polycarp's wisdom as useful to believers of every time and place. The same applies to a much greater degree to the letters of Paul, the particularity of which had to be superseded by universality to make them applicable.[9] In these circumstances

6. PolPhil 3–6 takes note of widows, deacons, and presbyters. How Polycarp knew about the structure of the community at Philippi is unknown. Such information may have been in the opening and/or closing of their letter(s), but he only addresses the entire adult male community.

7. For discussion see Pervo, "Acts in Ephesus (and Environs) c. 115," 146.

8. The cautious discussion of Hartog (*Polycarp's* Epistle), 40–45, indicates that internal evidence, if not unambiguous, inclines toward a later date. An emerging consensus that Ignatius fits the circumstances of c. 130 better than those of c. 115 dovetails with these data.

9. See Pervo, *The Making of Paul*, 23–61.

the preferable approach is not to assume that a hypothetical alternative to the unity of PolPhil exists, but to enquire which of the two hypotheses best accounts for the data. (This principle should be distinguished from the obligation to explain the present text by attempting to show where, how, when, and why it was edited into its present shape.) What are the data?

1. Since the mid-seventeenth century, if not since the fourth, readers of this letter have detected a problem of chronology. PolPhil 9 appears to assume that Ignatius and others have gone to their reward, but in chapter 13 Polycarp hopes that the Philippians can supply information about their fate. This is the single most glaring difficulty.

2. In 1:1 the future martyrs are mentioned but not named. 9:2 speaks of: "Ignatius, Zosimus, and Rufus . . . others from your community, and . . . Paul himself, as well as the other envoys." Zosimus and Rufus were not listed as companions of Ignatius in Smyrna and Troas (the latter of which was the final stop before Philippi). For 18 December the old Roman martyrology lists for commemoration: "At Philippi in Macedonia the birthday of holy martyrs Rufus and Zosimus, who were from that number of disciples through whom the primitive church was founded with Jews and Greeks, of the happy struggle of whom Saint Polycarp also [wrote] in the letter to the Philippians." The text of PolPhil treats them as a group, distinguished in this construction from the Philippian martyrs. The single-letter hypothesis gains support if "Ignatius and" [lit.] is deemed a later addition, although recent supporters of that hypothesis are reluctant to elect this option. Supporters of the two-letter hypothesis can argue that the language implies some distance between Ignatius' martyrdom and the present.

3. Verses 1:1–2 contain a grammatical gaffe. The two occasions of thanksgiving use different constructions. An English analogy is: "I heard you come in and that you went straight to the kitchen," rather than: "I heard you come in and go straight. . . ." Proponents of the two-letter hypothesis can propose that the first one of these was added when the letters were joined together, perhaps taking over the very words of the cover note. Their opponents can say that Polycarp is quite capable of such syntactical imperfection and/or that the text is corrupt.

4. When Eusebius incorporated chapter 13 into his history (*Hist. eccl.* 3.36.15), he omitted the last sentence: "As for Ignatius and his companions, please advise us if you learn anything definitive."[10] The best (which does not mean "the only") explanation for this phenomenon is that Eusebius, who laid

10. *Et de ipso Ignatio et de his qui cum eo sunt, quod certius agnoveritis, significate.*

Structure of Polycarp's Letter

Two-Letter Hypothesis		Single-Letter Hypothesis	
A. Cover Note for Ignatian Correspondence			
[1:1]	Epistolary Thanksgiving		
13	Body		
B. Response to Philippians' Request			
Inscription		Inscription	
1:2	Epistolary Thanksgiving	1:1–2	Epistolary Opening
2	Introduction to Body	2	Introduction to Body
3	Purpose: Correct Behavior	3	Purpose: Correct Behavior
4:1—6:3	Greed as Primary Example; Behavior in God's Household, with conclusion	4:1—6:3	Greed as Primary Example; Behavior in God's Household, with conclusion
7	Warning against Rival Teaching	7	Warning against Rival Teaching
8	Patient Endurance: Christ as Example	8	Patient Endurance: Christ as Example
9	Patient Endurance: Martyrs as Example	9	Patient Endurance: Martyrs as Example
10	Summary Advice	10	Summary Advice
11	The Case of Valens	11	The Case of Valens
12:1	Closing Admonition	12:1	Closing Admonition
12:2—14	Epistolary Closing:	12:2—14	Epistolary Closing:
12:2–3	Final Prayer	12:2–3	Final Prayer
		13	Ignatius & Ignatian Correspondence
14	Information about Agent, Final Blessing	14	Information about Agent, Final Blessing

the two chronological sections side by side, saw the discrepancy and passed over the final sentence.

5. In so far as is known, PolPhil did not circulate independently of the Ignatian correspondence, to which it is a fine companion piece. An editor at, for example, Philippi who wished to place this material into circulation might

well edit the cover note into the larger letter rather than discard it or retain it as a separate piece.[11] Various scenarios are conceivable, but retention of a short note as such would not have appeared to flatter Polycarp.

6. PolPhil 12 and 14 reflect the same pattern as 1 Clem 64–65: a final prayer that contains a catalogue of virtues and attributes to Christ the title "high priest," followed by remarks about the messengers and a closing blessing. Since Polycarp modeled the opening of his letter upon that of 1 Clement, it is not surprising that he should also do so at the close. PolPhil 13 disrupts this pattern. If, however, the letter is deemed a composite, the editor who inserted the cover note at this point acted rather intelligently.

7. Chapters 3 and 13 present two reasons for writing: "correct behavior" in the former and copies of Ignatius' letters in the latter. The two are not coordinated. Ideally, in chapter 13 Polycarp would mention that the Philippians had also made this request. The two purposes raise the possibility that the Philippians had written twice. One hypothesis is that Polycarp made a single answer to both requests. Another is that two responses have been merged.

This list indicates that a number of problems in PolPhil could be correlated to construct an argument for two letters. This does not seem to have happened. The premier attempt to explain the chronological conflict by proposing two letters was P. N. Harrison's 1936 *Polycarp's Two Epistles.* This is an engaging study of enduring value to all who study PolPhil, but those inclined toward the two-letter hypothesis no longer do so for Harrison's reasons alone, and refutation of his arguments cannot terminate the discussion. Harrison's object was to resolve the tension between the relatively early occasion of the letter, Ignatius' death c. 115, and material that seemed two decades later. Since proponents of the one-letter hypothesis now allow a later date, even if they do not recommend it, and since substantial advances have been made in questions of intertextuality and in other disciplines, cases for and against must rest upon different grounds.

The key task of proponents of the single-letter hypothesis is to harmonize chapter 9 with 13.[12] Advocates for two letters stress the contrast: The model for chapter 9 is 1 Clement 5, which looks back a good generation to the deaths of Peter and Paul, while in 13 Polycarp wants information about the

11. The current order of Ignatius' letters stems from Eusebius, *Hist. eccl.* 3.36. One witness, G, places Smyrnaeans and Polycarp first.

12. Michael Holmes did note that the dissonance in PolPhil 1 (3) could be the result of merging two letters, although he prefers the single-letter hypothesis, "Polycarp of Smyrna," 123.

fate of Ignatius. William Schoedel, whose brief commentary retains its worth after nearly a half-century, agrees that 9:2 refers to departed martyrs but holds that Ignatius, Zosimus, and Rufus are not included in this group, as v. 2 applies only to those in the "but also" clause.[13] This grammatical pleading constitutes a precarious base upon which to erect an argument. A stronger foundation appears in the adjective "blessed" (9:1), which, when joined to a proper name, means that the person is dead.[14]

13:2 exists only in Latin. Boudewijn Dehandschutter, a fine scholar of Polycarp, does not appear at his best in confronting this matter:

> Above all the interpretation of the thirteenth chapter must be revised: The closing words *et de ipso Ignatio et de his qui cum eo sunt, quod certius agnoveritis, significate* . . . [As for Ignatius and his companions, please advise us if you learn anything definitive] can be read as an unfortunate translation that implies the present tense, . . . even though this is not expressed in the Greek; the time perspective must thus not be changed with respect to chapter 9; in other words, chapter 13 does not assume Ignatius to still be living after all.[15]

The point in question is that a Greek retroversion could use a timeless participle. These verbal adjectives acquire temporal sense from the main verb in the indicative. Retroversions are not good bases for arguments because alternative translations are possible. (My own version avoids tense.) Note the flow of the argument: Dehandschutter first states how a retroverted text *can* be read. By the next sentence "can" becomes "must." Moreover he does not deal with Eusebius, who read the Greek original and apparently found this sentence unhelpful.[16] A better effort at harmonization is to posit that chapter 9 expected that death was in the offing while 13 shows that definitive news has not arrived.[17] This interpretation is possible and could support other evidence for unity, but what is possible is not therefore preferable.

Hartog calls for explanation of the missing epistolary opening and notes that Irenaeus and Eusebius, especially the latter, knew the letter in its current form.[18] A very solid majority of scholars regard 2 Corinthians as a

13. Schoedel, *Polycarp*, 28.

14. Spicq, *Theological Lexicon*, vol. 2, 434 and n. 9.

15. "Epistle of Polycarp," 121.

16. Attributing 13:2 to the Latin translator (see Dehandschutter, "Epistle of Polycarp," 121 and n. 28) is an unfalsifiable proposal for which no motive can be postulated. Barnard, "Problem," highlighted the significance of Eusebius' evident omission.

17. E.g., Schoedel, *Polycarp*, 40.

18. Hartog, *Polycarp's* Epistle, 36–37. In fact, 1:1 may contain part of that hypothetical opening. See Holmes, "Polycarp of Smyrna," 121.

composite of two or more letters, although the text never circulated other than in its present form, so far as is known, and grant that the amalgamation of letters must require altering beginnings and endings. Since proponents of the two-letter hypothesis can now grant that they may have been issued in close proximity, even a year or less, arguments based upon the appearance or absence of substantial temporal gaps are no longer useful. Finally, one does not refute an hypothesis by identifying alternatives to or weaknesses in its several points.

Neither side has put forth a compelling argument at this time. Any who wish to engage the matter anew should take into account the grounds for various partition hypotheses and strengthen their contribution with formal, redactional, and other parallels. Proposed solutions should solve more problems than they create and show how hypothetical partitions contribute to the understanding of a text. In this case the last will be rather minor. My translation therefore allows for both hypotheses.

6. Intertextuality

For works like the Apostolic Fathers, identification of sources serves a number of purposes. They may help date the work; more often these references date when various works were in circulation. Only once does Polycarp employ anything like a quotation formula (12:1), and he never names a source. Since he was evidently familiar with Matthew and Luke, who frequently mark quotations with formulae, the bishop's attitude is noteworthy.[19]

One almost has to argue that Polycarp was aware of the LXX. Again, his familiarity with Luke and Acts illustrates a path he chose not to follow. Conversely, Polycarp was enamored with 1 Peter and 1 Clement. One can imagine that he knew 1 Peter almost by heart and readily recalled it. Polycarp appears to stand at a juncture where written gospels are gaining in status over oral tradition (see 2:3 and comments). Citation of 1 John contrasts with ignorance/non-use of the fourth gospel. In 6:1, he uses what is normally a citation formula (lit., "knowing that"), followed by "we all stand in debt to sin." This suggests an unknown source, unless the bishop had reference to the Our Father. He evidently had a collection of Paul's epistles. In general, Polycarp views various early Christian writings as authoritative. He represents an incipient moment in the process of canonization. Legend features a confrontation between Polycarp and Marcion (Irenaeus, *Haer.*

19. For one survey of intertextuality in PolPhil, with references to others, see Hartog, *Polycarp's* Epistle, 53–65.

3.3.4). How should one imagine Marcion walking into Polycarp's shop, as it were, and demanding that they get rid of the Jewish Scriptures? "We don't use them as authoritative." The Gospel? "We have two in use (or three) and the living voice of Jesus." The Apostle? "We have Paul's letters. In addition we rely upon other fine texts." Their conversation would tie every history of the development of Christian doctrine into knots. Polycarp revered Paul, but his favorite sources come from the Pauline periphery: 1 Peter and 1 Clement. His preferences are late: Ephesians, cited for a moral lesson, dates 90–100, while the other two are from c. 100, and then come the even later Pastoral Epistles, which present a special case.

That case was pushed into the spotlight by Hans von Campenhausen, who proposed, in a piece first published in 1951, that Polycarp composed the PE.[20] Because the two are seldom read together, their similarities are widely overlooked. Both concern themselves with the Pauline legacy in western Asia Minor. 1 Timothy, Titus, and PolPhil are formally similar advisory epistles dealing with ecclesiastical matters. Only these two compositions—the PE understood here as a single-author project—combine the Household Code, found also in 1 Peter and 1 Clement, with a Church Order. The motive for this is ecclesiological: the church as the household of God, explicit in the PE, implicit in Polycarp. Each has a relatively detailed section on widows. To this amalgam the texts add ethical advice and critique of rival teaching.

Terms and methods exhibit striking similarities. Both view pastors as primarily teachers, whose task is to maintain/guard/protect the tradition they have received against false teaching. Both view greed as a central moral issue. PolPhil 4:1 is clearly dependent upon 1 Tim 6:7, 10. Both see a place for the church in society yet urge the endurance of suffering. Each repeats traditional Pauline statements about salvation but holds that good works are necessary. Linguistic similarities are numerous and can be quite precise.[21] Campenhausen concluded that the Pastor was a twin of Polycarp.[22]

Perhaps in the sense that Minneapolis and Saint Paul are "twin cities," that is, contiguous but dissimilar.[23] At their cores, the two authors have different theologies. The PE promote an "Epiphany Christology" accessorized with language from the ruler cult, centered around the two manifestations of Christ. Polycarp has none of this. He stresses Christ's past sacrificial death

20. "Polykarp von Smyrna und die Pastoralbriefe."

21. "Polykarp von Smyrna und die Pastoralbriefe," 221.

22. "Polykarp von Smyrna und die Pastoralbriefe," 252, to which I should add the parallel technique of 1 Tim 5:18 and PolPhil 12:1.

23. The author lives in St. Paul, has worked in Minneapolis, and is an identical twin.

and future role as judge. The PE show some literary artistry and creativity in their arrangement, with few but vivid images and a number of memorable phrases. PolPhil exhibits no artistic or creative interest. His lack of these qualities becomes, in the end, a strength. Moreover, Polycarp displays a fine pastoral sense and is eager to restrain judgmental approaches. The Pastor neither had such sense nor wished to gain it. He was concerned for the clergy, but not overflowing with mercy with regard to the faithful. These three differences receive attention because they are not matters that people are likely to utilize from time to time, among others. They are fundamental traits of character, temperament, and intellectual orientation.[24]

Campenhausen and others have shown that the PE and PolPhil come from a similar environment, exhibit similar understandings of ecclesiology and ethics, hold a common view of tradition, a similar orientation to the Christian past and to the pastoral task. If Polycarp wrote several decades after the Pastor, he was remarkably out of date. Avant-garde he was most certainly not, but for him, as for the Pastor, the good old days were the apostolic era. Comparison makes it difficult to attempt to date the PE earlier than 120. Circa 125 is a reasonable date. The most important result of this comparative study is to proclaim the merits of reading the PE and PolPhil together. That comparison is the object this edition seeks to achieve.

7. Theology

Since the text is quite brief and much of its theology emerges in conventional phrases of early Christian letters, all theological judgments are subject to qualification. The primary role of God is to beget Jesus Christ. Creation is largely ignored. God is all-seeing (7:2), responds to human prayer, and raises the faithful departed. About the Spirit Polycarp is silent. Empowerment comes from Christ's atoning act; thereafter, one is to imitate good examples.

Christology subsumes pneumatology. Atonement inaugurates new life. Were Christ's suffering not real, it would not have been effective or exemplary. Rejection of Docetism (the belief that Christ merely appeared to be human) does not therefore require pre-existence or incarnation. Christology and soteriology exist on two levels: Christ's suffering brought salvation, and those who embrace this deliverance will follow Christ's example. In so far as the text reveals, these two are not coordinated. This reinforces Polycarp's

24. For critiques of Campenhausen's proposal see Rensberger, "As the Apostle Teaches," 170–74, and, in detail, Merz, *Fiktive*, 114–40.

comfort with the periphery of Deuteropauline thought. His appreciation of 1 Clement is supplemented by the Pastor's Paulinism, but the conflicts behind Galatians and Romans are of limited relevance.

Polycarp's ethical ideas are not original, a judgment that he would take as a compliment. As indicated elsewhere, "righteousness" most often refers to doing the right thing. The primary function of eschatology relates to fear of individual judgment. Cosmic elements are ignored. Although he does not have a pessimistic anthropology that stresses the dominance of sin, he is fully aware of human weakness and views caution in issuing judgments and readiness to forgive as among the greatest of spiritual gifts. If appreciation of love was the only concept of Paul's that he took to heart, he could have done worse—as more than a few have. What holds Polycarp's theology together is not cohesion among Christology, soteriology, ecclesiology/sacramental theology, and eschatology, but sound and well-rounded pastoral sense.

Salvation history gets no more than a bit part in his transition to polemics (6:3). General denunciations of deceivers are common in the PE (1 Tim 6:10; 2 Tim 3:13; Titus 3:3), Ignatius (e.g. Eph 16:1), and elsewhere. The rejection of Docetism in 7:1 is based upon 1 John 4:2–3, but also found in Ignatius (relevantly: IgnSm 1; 2; 5:2). Denial of resurrection is reminiscent of 2 Tim 2:18. Polycarp does not echo the common early Christian association of false teaching with the last times. It is difficult to claim that rival teachings are more than boilerplate for Polycarp, at least in relation to his concerns for those at Philippi.

8. Date

Explicit proximity to the death of Ignatius establishes 130–35 as a reasonable time-frame for both the single and the two-letter hypotheses. This dating also accords with Polycarp's knowledge and appreciation of early Christian literature.

9. Reception and Influence

In comparison to stories about his life and the account of his martyrdom, the impact of Polycarp's correspondence has been quite minimal. Today it is valued as a monument of pastoral guidance in an important era.

POLYCARP TO THE PHILIPPIANS

Cover Note (Two-Letter Hypothesis)

13 Ἐγράψατέ μοι καὶ ὑμεῖς καὶ Ἰγνάτιος ἵν' ἐάν τις ἀπέρχηται εἰς Συρίαν καὶ τὰ παρ' ὑμῶν ἀποκομίσῃ γράμματα ὅπερ ποιήσω ἐὰν λάβω καιρὸν εὔθετον εἴτε ἐγώ εἴτε ὃν πέμπω πρεσβεύσοντα καὶ περὶ ὑμῶν [2]τὰς ἐπιστολὰς Ἰγνατίου τὰς πεμφθείσας ἡμῖν ὑπ' αὐτοῦ καὶ ἄλλας ὅσας εἴχομεν παρ' ἡμῖν ἐπέμψαμεν ὑμῖν καθὼς ἐνετείλασθε αἵτινες ὑποτεταγμέναι εἰσὶν τῇ ἐπιστολῇ ταύτῃ ἐξ ὧν μεγάλα ὠφεληθῆναι δυνήσεσθε περιέχουσι γὰρ πίστιν καὶ ὑπομονὴν καὶ πᾶσαν οἰκοδομὴν τὴν εἰς τὸν κύριον ἡμῶν ἀνήκουσαν. Et de ipso Ignatio et de his qui cum eo sunt, quod certius agnoveritis, significate.

Epistolary Opening

1 Πολύκαρπος καὶ οἱ σὺν αὐτῷ πρεσβύτεροι τῇ ἐκκλησίᾳ τοῦ θεοῦ τῇ παροικούσῃ Φιλίππους ἔλεος ὑμῖν καὶ εἰρήνη παρὰ θεοῦ παντοκράτορος καὶ Ἰησοῦ Χριστοῦ τοῦ σωτῆρος ἡμῶν πληθυνθείη

Epistolary Thanksgiving

Συνεχάρην ὑμῖν μεγάλως ἐν τῷ κυρίῳ ἡμῶν Ἰησοῦ Χριστῷ δεξαμένοις τὰ μιμήματα τῆς ἀληθοῦς ἀγάπης καὶ προπέμψασιν ὡς ἐπέβαλεν ὑμῖν τοὺς ἐνειλημένους τοῖς ἁγιοπρεπέσιν δεσμοῖς ἅτινά ἐστιν διαδήματα τῶν ἀληθῶς ὑπὸ θεοῦ καὶ τοῦ κυρίου ἡμῶν ἐκλελεγμένων [2]καὶ ὅτι ἡ βεβαία τῆς πίστεως ὑμῶν ῥίζα ἐξ ἀρχαίων καταγγελλομένη χρόνων μέχρι νῦν διαμένει καὶ καρποφορεῖ εἰς τὸν κύριον ἡμῶν Ἰησοῦν Χριστόν ὃς ὑπέμεινεν ὑπὲρ τῶν ἁμαρτιῶν ἡμῶν ἕως θανάτου καταντῆσαι ὃν ἤγειρεν ὁ θεός λύσας τὰς ὠδῖνας τοῦ ᾅδου [3]εἰς ὃν οὐκ ἰδόντες πιστεύετε χαρᾷ ἀνεκλαλήτῳ

- **13** Eusebius (*Hist. eccl.* 3.36.14–15) preserves this text in Greek, except for the last sentence. The best explanation for this omission is that the church historian perceived that it was at variance with chap. 9, from which he had just quoted. From chap. 9 readers gather that Ignatius was a martyr. 13.2 implies that news about him had not yet reached Smyrna. See the Introduction under "Unity." This brief paragraph underlines the nature of private communication in antiquity. Correspondence was sent by hand. The rich might delegate this task to a slave, but others had to wait for someone who planned to go to that destination or undertake the task personally. Chapter 13 also illustrates the interest in and means for collecting letters. See 1 Thess 5:27; Col 4:16.
- **13:1** On Ignatius' interest in Polycarp's travel, see IgnSm 11:2; PolPhil 7:2.
- **13:2** Although he happily shares Ignatius' letters, the bishop of Smyrna does not hesitate to tell his readers what they contain. One would not easily gather that Ignatius reveled in dazzling rhetoric, exhibited a vigorous theology, and viewed order as the path to unity. In short, the sentence says more

Cover Note (Two-Letter Hypothesis)

13 Both you and Ignatius wrote me that anyone going to Syria should also convey your letter. This I shall do if a suitable opportunity arises—either in person or through a representative I dispatch on behalf of you as well as myself. [2]In addition we are enclosing the letters of Ignatius that he sent us and others in our possession, as you directed. You will find them highly profitable, as they contain material dealing with trust and patience under stress and everything leading to growth in our master. As for Ignatius and his companions, please advise us if you learn anything definitive.

Epistolary Opening

1 Polycarp and his *presbyters* to God's expatriate community at Philippi: May you overflow with compassion and wellbeing from almighty God and Jesus Christ our deliverer.

Epistolary Thanksgiving

When you welcomed the reflections of genuine affection and properly sent on their way those bedecked in chains suitable for God's own, the regal head bands of those truly chosen by God and our master, I was as happy in the Christian life as you were. [2]Another source of joy is that your deeply rooted trust, renowned from the earliest times, still thrives and continues to produce fruit for our master Jesus Christ, who for our shortcomings endured to the death. God raised him, shattering the fetters of Hell. [3]Although you have not seen him, you trust with inexpressible and splendid joy—a joy that many have longed to possess, since you know that you are

---

about Polycarp's priorities than those of Ignatius.

- **1:1** closely follows the inscription of 1 Clement. *His presbyters.* Polycarp writes as a bishop, supported by a council of presbyters. He writes to the entire community. No officers are named. Polycarp may prefer to name none. The former bishop may have been Valens (chaps. 11–12), or the community may not have had episcopal organization at this time.
- **1:2** Cf. 1 Clem 1:2. *Fetters of Hell.* Cf. Acts 2:24, the textual variants of which include both "Death" and "Hades."
- **1:2–3** The translation smooths over grammatical irregularities which might come from the fusing of two letters. See the Introduction under "Unity."
- **1:3** Cf. 1 Clem 32.3–4. *Inexpressible and splendid joy*. This depends upon 1 Pet 1:8. *Since you know that* is a citation formula, introducing parts of Eph 2:5, 8, 9. Although the language comes from the secondary tradition, Polycarp's soteriology is closer to Luke's. Forgiveness, brought through Christ's death, cleans the slate. Believers should thereafter live virtuous lives on their own.

καὶ δεδοξασμένῃ εἰς ἣν πολλοὶ ἐπιθυμοῦσιν εἰσελθεῖν εἰδότες ὅτι χάριτί ἐστε σεσωσμένοι οὐκ ἐξ ἔργων ἀλλὰ θελήματι θεοῦ διὰ Ἰησοῦ Χριστοῦ.

Threat and Promise

2 Διὸ ἀναζωσάμενοι τὰς ὀσφύας ὑμῶν δουλεύσατε τῷ θεῷ ἐν φόβῳ καὶ ἀληθείᾳ ἀπολιπόντες τήν κενὴν ματαιολογίαν καὶ τὴν τῶν πολλῶν πλάνην πιστεύσαντες εἰς τὸν ἐγείραντα τὸν κύριον ἡμῶν Ἰησοῦν Χριστὸν ἐκ νεκρῶν καὶ δόντα αὐτῷ δόξαν καὶ θρόνον ἐκ δεξιῶν αὐτοῦ ᾧ ὑπετάγη τὰ πάντα ἐπουράνια καὶ ἐπίγεια ᾧ πᾶσα πνοὴ λατρεύει ὃς ἔρχεται κριτὴς ζώντων καὶ νεκρῶν οὗ τὸ αἷμα ἐκζητήσει ὁ θεὸς ἀπὸ τῶν ἀπειθούντων αὐτῷ [2]ὁ δὲ ἐγείρας αὐτὸν ἐκ νεκρῶν καὶ ἡμᾶς ἐγερεῖ ἐὰν ποιῶμεν αὐτοῦ τὸ θέλημα καὶ πορευώμεθα ἐν ταῖς ἐντολαῖς αὐτοῦ καὶ ἀγαπῶμεν ἃ ἠγάπησεν ἀπεχόμενοι πάσης ἀδικίας πλεονεξίας φιλαργυρίας καταλαλιᾶς ψευδομαρτυρίας μὴ ἀποδιδόντες κακὸν ἀντὶ κακοῦ ἢ λοιδορίαν ἀντὶ λοιδορίας ἢ γρόνθον ἀντὶ γρόνθου ἢ κατάραν ἀντὶ κατάρας [3]μνημονεύοντες δὲ ὧν εἶπεν ὁ κύριος διδάσκων Μὴ κρίνετε ἵνα μὴ κριθῆτε ἀφίετε καὶ ἀφεθήσεται ὑμῖν ἐλεᾶτε ἵνα ἐλεηθῆτε ᾧ μέτρῳ μετρεῖτε ἀντιμετρηθήσεται ὑμῖν καὶ ὅτι μακάριοι οἱ πτωχοὶ καὶ οἱ διωκόμενοι ἕνεκεν δικαιοσύνης ὅτι αὐτῶν ἐστὶν ἡ βασιλεία τοῦ θεοῦ.

Purpose: Correct Behavior

3 Ταῦτα ἀδελφοί οὐκ ἐμαυτῷ ἐπιτρέψας γράφω ὑμῖν περὶ τῆς
Paul δικαιοσύνης ἀλλ' ἐπεὶ ὑμεῖς προεπεκαλέσασθέ με [2]οὔτε γὰρ ἐγὼ οὔτε
ἄλλος ὅμοιος ἐμοὶ δύναται κατακολουθῆσαι τῇ σοφίᾳ τοῦ μακαρίου

3:1 *Invited* is a conjecture for nonsensical terms in the mss.

- **2:1** *Roll up.* A more literal version would be "hike up your skirts." The metaphor refers to appropriate attire for hard labor. For the phrases see 1 Pet 1:13; Psa 2:11; 1 Clem 19:1. *Shallow, superficial chatter* derives from 1 Tim 1:6; cf. also Titus 1:10. The language refers to idolatry and, by extension, to rival Christian teachings.
- **2:2** Like the Pastor, Polycarp views good works as necessary for ultimate salvation. The vice list (see Titus 1:6) is like that of 1 Clem 35:5, with the addition of greed. This and the judgment saying prepare for the issues of chaps. 10–11. On Christ as judge, see 2 Tim 4:2. *Not repaying . . . slander* comes from 1 Pet 3:9. Cf. also Matt 5:39; Luke 6:28–29.
- **2:3** Polycarp bases the exhortation to refrain from judgment upon Christ's future role, unlike the Sermon on the Mount. Using an introductory formula for citing Jesus-sayings, Polycarp cites 1 Clem 13:1–2 on judgment, but his

delivered by generosity, not from what you accomplish but by God's intention through Jesus Christ.

Threat and Promise

2 Therefore roll up your sleeves and serve God with genuine reverence. Abandon the shallow, superficial chatter and error of the multitude for trust in the one who raised our master Jesus Christ from the dead, endowed him with splendor and the place of honor, and subjected to him everything celestial and terrestrial. Every animate creature worships Christ. He will come as judge of the living and the dead. God will charge the disobedient with responsibility for Jesus' death. [2]The one who raised him from the dead will also raise us if we do what he wishes, follow his rules and cherish what Jesus cherished as we discard every species of wrongdoing, greed, lust for money, malicious gossip, and prevaricating, not repaying evil with evil, slander with slander, blow with blow, or curse with curse. [3]Keep in mind what the master taught: "Don't judge so that you won't be judged; forgive and be forgiven. The criteria you utilized will be applied to you." And "Congratulations to the poor and those persecuted for doing right, because God's domain belongs to them."

Purpose: Correct Behavior

3 It was not my idea, brothers and sisters, to write these observations about correct behavior to you, but because you invited me to do so. [2]Neither I nor anyone at my level could walk in the shoes of the blessed and glorious Paul. When he was with your community

Paul

---

phrasing shows the influence of Matt 7:1–2//Luke 6:36–38. He knew both gospels but did not view them as normative sources. Compare and contrast the Pastor: 1 Tim 5:18.

- **3:1** *Correct behavior* forms a bracket (*inclusio*) around this chapter. The term has little of Paul's sense of "righteousness," an apocalyptic term for God's vindication of justice. Polycarp states that the Philippians requested his wisdom on the matter. Although he reveres Paul, he does not reiterate Paul's theology of justification because it was no longer relevant. It is possible that some known to the Philippians were attempting to maintain the Pauline view. The immediate problem was Valens' incorrect behavior. For Polycarp righteousness is sound behavior, repeatedly exemplified.
- **3:2** *Blessed* (*makarios*) is acquiring a technical sense. *Letters* need not refer to more than one. Canonical Philippians may be a composite, but Polycarp would have known it from the collection of Pauline correspondence, where it was a single piece.

καὶ ἐνδόξου Παύλου ὃς γενόμενος ἐν ὑμῖν κατὰ πρόσωπον τῶν τότε ἀνθρώπων ἐδίδαξεν ἀκριβῶς καὶ βεβαίως τὸν περὶ ἀληθείας λόγον ὃς καὶ ἀπὼν ὑμῖν ἔγραψεν ἐπιστολάς εἰς ἃς ἐὰν ἐγκύπτητε δυνηθήσεσθε οἰκοδομεῖσθαι εἰς τὴν δοθεῖσαν ὑμῖν πίστιν [3]ἥτις ἐστὶν μήτηρ πάντων ἡμῶν ἐπακολουθούσης τῆς ἐλπίδος προαγούσης τῆς ἀγάπης τῆς εἰς θεὸν καὶ Χριστόν καὶ εἰς τὸν πλησίον ἐὰν γάρ τις τούτων ἐντὸς ᾖ πεπλήρωκεν ἐντολὴν δικαιοσύνης ὁ γὰρ ἔχων ἀγάπην μακράν ἐστιν πάσης ἁμαρτίας.

Rules for God's Household

4 Ἀρχὴ δὲ πάντων χαλεπῶν φιλαργυρία εἰδότες οὖν ὅτι οὐδὲν εἰσηνέγκαμεν εἰς τὸν κόσμον ἀλλ᾽ οὐδὲ ἐξενεγκεῖν τι ἔχομεν ὁπλισώμεθα τοῖς ὅπλοις τῆς δικαιοσύνης καὶ διδάξωμεν ἑαυτοὺς

Wives πρῶτον πορεύεσθαι ἐν τῇ ἐντολῇ τοῦ κυρίου [2]ἔπειτα καὶ τὰς γυναῖκας ἡμῶν ἐν τῇ δοθείσῃ αὐταῖς πίστει καὶ ἀγάπῃ καὶ ἁγνείᾳ στεργούσας τοὺς ἑαυτῶν ἄνδρας ἐν πάσῃ ἀληθείᾳ καὶ ἀγαπώσας πάντας ἐξ ἴσου ἐν πάσῃ ἐγκρατείᾳ καὶ τὰ τέκνα παιδεύειν τὴν παιδείαν τοῦ φόβου τοῦ θεοῦ [3]τὰς χήρας σωφρονούσας περὶ τὴν τοῦ κυρίου πίστιν ἐντυγχανούσας ἀδιαλείπτως περὶ πάντων μακρὰν οὔσας πάσης διαβολῆς καταλαλιᾶς ψευδομαρτυρίας φιλαργυρίας καὶ παντὸς κακοῦ γινωσκούσας ὅτι εἰσὶ θυσιαστήριον θεοῦ καὶ ὅτι πάντα μωμοσκοπεῖται καὶ λέληθεν αὐτὸν οὐδὲν οὔτε λογισμῶν οὔτε ἐννοιῶν οὔτε τι τῶν κρυπτῶν τῆς καρδίας.

5 Εἰδότες οὖν ὅτι θεὸς οὐ μυκτηρίζεται ὀφείλομεν ἀξίως τῆς

Deacons ἐντολῆς αὐτοῦ καὶ δόξης περιπατεῖν [2]ὁμοίως διάκονοι ἄμεμπτοι κατενώπιον αὐτοῦ τῆς δικαιοσύνης ὡς θεοῦ καὶ Χριστοῦ διάκονοι

- **3:3** is built upon the triad of faith, hope, and love. For faith as *mother* see *Martyrdom of Justin* 4.8. The most dramatic form of the closing words is Augustine's "Love and do what you want" (*Treatise on 1 John* 7.8).
- **4:1** The sentiment is widespread, but the second clause, introduced with a citation formula, derives from 1 Tim 6:7, establishing that the proverb is from 1 Tim 6:10. Polycarp seems to improve the construction. As does the Pastor (1 Tim 6:3–5, 10, 11; Titus 1:11), Polycarp tends to link greed to rival theologies; cf. 11:2. This was a venerable weapon of the polemical tool chest.
  Weapons. See 2 Cor 6:7 (cf. Rom 13:12; Eph 6:13). For Paul these are instruments bestowed by redemption. Polycarp views them as virtues to be utilized. This image introduces the Household Code. Unreflectively patriarchal, Polycarp begins with "us," male heads of the household, whose duties are summarized in obedience to Christ's command. This may be the love commandment. They will instruct wives and widows.
- **4:2** For wives ritual purity replaces "hope" in the traditional triad. Childrearing is the women's responsibility. See 1 Clem 1:3; 21:6–7.

as then constituted in person, he made an accurate and reliable presentation of the message about the truth. When absent he wrote you letters that, when you dig deeply into them, will be able to fortify you in the trust bestowed upon you. [3]This trust is the mother of all of us. Hope follows, while affection directed toward God, Christ, and our fellow humans leads. Whoever moves in this company has met the demand for correct behavior, for having affection makes one distant from all misdoing.

Rules for God's Household

4 Troubles of every variety stem from the pursuit of wealth. Since, then, we realize that we brought nothing into the world and can take nothing out, let us equip ourselves with the weapons of correct behavior. Our primary task is to show ourselves how to follow the master's rule. [2]Next we must instruct our wives to continue in the trust, affection, and purity bestowed upon them, cherishing their husbands with utter sincerity, bestowing equal and incontestably chaste affection upon all, and disciplining their children to teach them reverence for God. [3]We must instruct the widows to practice the faith with discretion, always making intercession for everyone and staying far from slander, malicious gossip, prevarication, lust for money, in short, evil of every sort, since they realize that they are God's altar and that all offerings are carefully scrutinized for blemishes, and that nothing eludes God, neither thoughts nor intentions nor deeply held secrets.

Wives

5 Because we know that God can't be fooled, we ought to conduct ourselves in ways that befit God's directive and majesty. [2]For *deacons* this means being blameless from the perspective of correct

Deacons

- **4:3** Widows are viewed primarily as an ecclesiastical rather than a family group. Polycarp understands the metaphor *altar* to apply to their offering of prayer. The catalogue of vices and implicit admonitions suggests that widows worry him no less than they do the Pastor. See 1 Clem 30:3; 41:2; 21:3.
- **5** An inclusion ("conduct oneself") frames the chapter. Polycarp continues to interlace domestic and ecclesiastical roles. This is intentional.
- **5:1** A formula introduces a citation of Gal 6:7. As in 4:1, the general principle is obedience to God's command, strengthened with a reference to divine transcendence.
- **5:2** The duties of *deacons* are based upon 1 Tim 3:1–13. The model, as often in Ignatius, is Christological, with the synoptic "servant (*diakonos*) of all." *In this age*, *slanderous*, *insincere*, and *self-controlled* appear only in the PE; cf. also 1 Clem 21:1. The second half of the verse appears to be a general *quid pro quo* promise.

καὶ οὐκ ἀνθρώπων μὴ διάβολοι μὴ δίλογοι ἀφιλάργυροι ἐγκρατεῖς περὶ πάντα εὔσπλαγχνοι ἐπιμελεῖς πορευόμενοι κατὰ τὴν ἀλήθειαν τοῦ κυρίου ὃς ἐγένετο διάκονος πάντων ᾧ ἐὰν εὐαρεστήσωμεν ἐν τῷ νῦν αἰῶνι ἀποληψόμεθα καὶ τὸν μέλλοντα καθὼς ὑπέσχετο ἡμῖν ἐγεῖραι ἡμᾶς ἐκ νεκρῶν καὶ ὅτι ἐὰν πολιτευσώμεθα ἀξίως αὐτοῦ καὶ συμβασιλεύσομεν αὐτῷ εἴγε πιστεύομεν

Young Men

[3]ὁμοίως καὶ νεώτεροι ἄμεμπτοι ἐν πᾶσιν πρὸ παντὸς προνοοῦντες ἁγνείας καὶ χαλιναγωγοῦντες ἑαυτοὺς ἀπὸ παντὸς κακοῦ καλὸν γὰρ τὸ ἀνακόπτεσθαι ἀπὸ τῶν ἐπιθυμιῶν ἐν τῷ κόσμῳ ὅτι πᾶσα ἐπιθυμία κατὰ τοῦ πνεύματος στρατεύεται καὶ οὔτε πόρνοι οὔτε μαλακοὶ οὔτε ἀρσενοκοῖται βασιλείαν θεοῦ κληρονομήσουσιν οὔτε οἱ ποιοῦντες τὰ ἄτοπα διὸ δέον ἀπέχεσθαι ἀπὸ πάντων τούτων ὑποτασσομένους τοῖς πρεσβυτέροις καὶ διακόνοις ὡς θεῷ καὶ Χριστῷ

Young Women

τὰς παρθένους ἐν ἀμώμῳ καὶ ἁγνῇ συνειδήσει περιπατεῖν

Presbyters

6 Καὶ οἱ πρεσβύτεροι δὲ εὔσπλαγχνοι εἰς πάντας ἐλεήμονες ἐπιστρέφοντες τὰ ἀποπεπλανημένα ἐπισκεπτόμενοι πάντας ἀσθενεῖς μὴ ἀμελοῦντες χήρας ἢ ὀρφανοῦ ἢ πένητος ἀλλὰ προνοοῦντες ἀεὶ τοῦ καλοῦ ἐνώπιον θεοῦ καὶ ἀνθρώπων ἀπεχόμενοι πάσης ὀργῆς προσωποληψίας κρίσεως ἀδίκου μακρὰν ὄντες πάσης φιλαργυρίας μὴ ταχέως πιστεύοντες κατά τινος μὴ ἀπότομοι ἐν κρίσει εἰδότες ὅτι πάντες ὀφειλέται ἐσμὲν ἁμαρτίας.

Concluding Exhortation

[2]εἰ οὖν δεόμεθα τοῦ κυρίου ἵνα ἡμῖν ἀφῇ ὀφείλομεν καὶ ἡμεῖς ἀφιέναι ἀπέναντι γὰρ τῶν τοῦ κυρίου καὶ θεοῦ ἐσμὲν ὀφθαλμῶν καὶ πάντας δεῖ παραστῆναι τῷ βήματι τοῦ Χριστοῦ καὶ ἕκαστον ὑπὲρ αὐτοῦ λόγον δοῦναι [3]οὕτως οὖν δουλεύσωμεν αὐτῷ μετὰ φόβου καὶ πάσης εὐλαβείας καθὼς αὐτὸς ἐνετείλατο καὶ οἱ εὐαγγελισάμενοι

6:3 *Message to us.* The variant "you" is dramatically effective but less probable. See 7:2.

- **5:3** A major concern for young men is sexual conduct. Polycarp was not the first to hit upon this idea. He utilizes the catalogue from 1 Cor 6:9–10. Same-sex activity was promoted by segregation of the sexes and the life of the gymnasium. Young women receive a general but comprehensive edict. The basis is evidently 1 Clem 1:3. On *conscience* see 1 Tim 1:5, 19; 3:9; 4:2.
- **6** Note once more that Polycarp omits the *bishop/bishops* from his discussion. *Presbyters'* duties center around pastoral care, including judgment about misconduct. Polycarp's thoughts are on the Valens situation of chaps. 10–11. As elsewhere Polycarp is at his pastoral best in urging forgiveness of others, restraint in judgment, and moderation.

behavior, because they are servants of God and Christ, not of mortals. They are not to be slanderous, insincere, or greedy; rather they should be self-disciplined, living by the master's truth. He became the servant of all. Pleasing him in this age means participating in the age to come, as he promised us, that he would raise us from the dead, and that, if we conduct ourselves as he would, we shall share his rule—provided that we continue to place our trust in him.

Young Men

[3]The young men also are to be absolutely blameless. Purity is to be their primary concern; they must restrain themselves from all evil. It is good to abstain from worldly desires, because every desire is in conflict with the spirit. Neither the sexually immoral, nor males who are passive or active sexual partners with other men, nor those who engage in any sexual improprieties will inherit God's domain. Young men must abstain from all these acts and be obedient to the *presbyters* and *deacons* as to God and Christ.

Young Women

Young women should conduct themselves with an undefiled and pure conscience.

Presbyters

6 As for *presbyters*, they should be well-disposed toward all, compassionate, bringing back the wayward, visiting all the sick, not neglecting widows, orphans, and the poor, constantly striving for what is good from both the divine and human perspective. They should avoid anger completely, partiality, and unfair judgment. Not even the suspicion of greed should come near them. They should be neither quick to accept accusations against people nor harsh in judgment, since they know that we all stand in debt to sin.

Concluding Exhortation

[2]Since we ask the master to forgive us, we too must be forgiving, for we are all under the eyes of the master and God and must all stand before Christ's bench, where each must render a personal account. [3]Let us, in consequence, serve Christ with total reverential awe, as he directed, as did the apostles who brought the great mes-

---

- **6:1** Allusions to 1 Tim 4:14; 5:9, 19; 6:10; Titus 1:13; 1 Pet 2:25; 5:2; and 1 Clem 13:1 are arguably perceptible. The final reference to sin comes from an unknown source, although the Our Father may be in mind.
- **6:2** *Bench*. Cf. Rom 14:10; 2 Cor 5:10, where manuscript evidence for both "God's" and "Christ's" can be found.
- **6:3** *Prophets* refers to those identified by Luke (e.g. Acts 3:18), without specificity. Polycarp has no need to cite passages. The closing is a transition to the subject of chap. 7.

ἡμᾶς ἀπόστολοι καὶ οἱ προφῆται οἱ προκηρύξαντες τὴν ἔλευσιν τοῦ κυρίου ἡμῶν ζηλωταὶ περὶ τὸ καλόν ἀπεχόμενοι τῶν σκανδάλων καὶ τῶν ψευδαδέλφων καὶ τῶν ἐν ὑποκρίσει φερόντων τὸ ὄνομα τοῦ κυρίου οἵτινες ἀποπλανῶσι κενοὺς ἀνθρώπους.

False & True Teaching

Docetism

7 Πᾶς γὰρ ὃς ἂν μὴ ὁμολογῇ Ἰησοῦν Χριστὸν ἐν σαρκὶ ἐληλυθέναι ἀντιχριστός ἐστιν καὶ ὃς ἂν μὴ ὁμολογῇ τὸ μαρτύριον τοῦ σταυροῦ ἐκ τοῦ διαβόλου ἐστίν καὶ ὃς ἂν μεθοδεύῃ τὰ λόγια τοῦ κυρίου πρὸς τὰς ἰδίας ἐπιθυμίας καὶ λέγῃ μήτε ἀνάστασιν μήτε κρίσιν οὗτος πρωτότοκος ἐστι τοῦ σατανᾶ.

[2]διὸ ἀπολιπόντες τὴν ματαιότητα τῶν πολλῶν καὶ τὰς ψευδοδιδασκαλίας ἐπὶ τὸν ἐξ ἀρχῆς ἡμῖν παραδοθέντα λόγον ἐπιστρέψωμεν νήφοντες πρὸς τὰς εὐχὰς καὶ προσκαρτεροῦντες νηστείαις δεήσεσιν αἰτούμενοι τὸν παντεπόπτην θεὸν μὴ εἰσενεγκεῖν ἡμᾶς εἰς πειρασμόν καθὼς εἶπεν ὁ κύριος τὸ μὲν πνεῦμα πρόθυμον ἡ δὲ σὰρξ ἀσθενής.

Example 1: Christ

8 Ἀδιαλείπτως οὖν προσκαρτερῶμεν τῇ ἐλπίδι ἡμῶν καὶ τῷ ἀρραβῶνι τῆς δικαιοσύνης ἡμῶν ὅς ἐστι Χριστὸς Ἰησοῦς

> ὃς ἀνήνεγκεν ἡμῶν τὰς ἁμαρτίας τῷ ἰδίῳ σώματι ἐπὶ τὸ ξύλον
> ὃς ἁμαρτίαν οὐκ ἐποίησεν
> οὐδὲ εὑρέθη δόλος ἐν τῷ στόματι αὐτοῦ

- 7 Polycarp does not appear to have received any information about rival teaching in Philippi, nor does he link the views identified in this chapter with his major themes. Rebuffed are Docetism—the view that Jesus only appeared to be human—and an eschatology like that opposed by the Pastor in 2 Tim 2:18. These views are not linked together nor do they conform to any known system.
- **7:1** The basis of the rejection of Docetism is 1 John 4:2–3. Polycarp follows 1 John in "demythologizing" the notion of the Antichrist, who is now a human teacher of doctrine Polycarp rejects. *Message of the cross* may be linked to 1 John 5:6–8. Ignatius appealed to the cross against docetists in IgnSm 1:1–2; cf. IgnTr 9–11. Polycarp testifies to the utility and acceptance of 1 John before the Gospel in circles that would prevail. The epistle(s) provided the hermeneutical key for understanding and thus accepting the Fourth Gospel. *Manipulating the master's pronouncements* (*logia*) probably refers to written collections. The verb could refer to interpretation or, slightly less likely, to alteration. Personal motivation is a common charge; cf. 2 Pet 3:3, 14–16. The epithet *belongs to the adversary* is Johannine in form. Cf. 1 John 3:3. *Satan's favorite child* is an old weapon of religious opprobrium. This may be the source of the anecdote that Polycarp called Marcion "Satan's firstborn" (Irenaeus, *Haer.* 3.3.4).

sage to us, as well as the prophets who announced in advance the master's coming. Let us be ardent in pursuit of the good and distant from potentially troublesome situations, as well as from false believers and any who call themselves Christians under false pretenses and deceive senseless people.

False & True Teaching

Docetism

7 Everyone who will not affirm that Jesus Christ has come in the flesh is a pseudo-messiah; whoever will not accept the message of the cross belongs to the adversary; and anyone who manipulates the master's pronouncements to suit personal interests and denies both resurrection and final judgment is Satan's favorite child.

2 Therefore let us abandon the inanity of the masses and false teachings and get back to the message originally transmitted to us. Let us be responsible in our prayers and regular in our fasting, begging God whom nothing eludes not to bring us to a great test of our faith. As the master said, "Though the spirit is willing, the flesh is weak."

Example 1: Christ

8 Let us never relax our grasp of the pledged hope of our vindication: the Anointed Jesus,

> who bore our failures on his body upon the cross;
> who did no wrong,
> spoke no deceit

- **7:2** Much in the manner of the Pastor, Polycarp urges adherence to the transmitted tradition; cf. 1 John 1:1–4 ("beginning"); 1 Clem 19:2. Despite *get back* he does not claim that his audience has forsaken this tradition. The idea that God sees all is a popular Greek notion; cf. 1 Clem 55:6; 64:1. The final words are shaped by the Gethsemane narrative: on *temptation*, see Matt 26:41; on *spirit . . . flesh*, contrast Matt 26:38. Polycarp shows that the Our Father was understood as referring to the great eschatological trial, not to ephemeral errors. For Polycarp fear of judgment was a great stimulus to the moral life. He was, alas, not the last to utilize that tenet.
- **8:1** 1 Peter 2:22–24 provides the material for this exhortation, which moves from the indicative (what Christ has done) to the imperative (what we can therefore do). For Paul the Spirit was a "pledge" (2 Cor 1:22; 5:5). *Vindication* renders Paul's "justification," usually translated here as "correct behavior." The version treats "hope and pledge of our vindication" as a hendyadis. The ball is now in our court. Christ has made the first payment. The rest is up to us. Rather than follow Christ believers are to imitate him. These are important shifts, but Polycarp stresses that Christ did not suffer so that we shall not have to. His Christology is less exemplarist than Luke's. One might label it "semi-exemplarist."

ἀλλὰ δι' ἡμᾶς ἵνα ζήσωμεν ἐν αὐτῷ πάντα ὑπέμεινεν
[2]μιμηταὶ οὖν γενώμεθα τῆς ὑπομονῆς αὐτοῦ
καὶ ἐὰν πάσχωμεν διὰ τὸ ὄνομα αὐτοῦ
δοξάζωμεν αὐτὸν τοῦτον γὰρ ἡμῖν τὸν ὑπογραμμὸν ἔθηκε δι' ἑαυτοῦ
καὶ ἡμεῖς τοῦτο ἐπιστεύσαμεν.

Example 2: The Martyrs

9 Παρακαλῶ οὖν πάντας ὑμᾶς πειθαρχεῖν τῷ λόγῳ τῆς δικαιοσύνης καὶ ἀσκεῖν πᾶσαν ὑπομονὴν ἣν καὶ εἴδατε κατ' ὀφθαλμοὺς οὐ μόνον ἐν τοῖς μακαρίοις Ἰγνατίῳ καὶ Ζωσίμῳ καὶ Ῥούφῳ ἀλλὰ καὶ ἐν ἄλλοις τοῖς ἐξ ὑμῶν καὶ ἐν αὐτῷ Παύλῳ καὶ τοῖς λοιποῖς ἀποστόλοις [2]πεπεισμένους ὅτι οὗτοι πάντες οὐκ εἰς κενὸν ἔδραμον ἀλλ' ἐν πίστει καὶ δικαιοσύνῃ καὶ ὅτι εἰς τὸν ὀφειλόμενον αὐτοῖς τόπον εἰσὶ παρὰ τῷ κυρίῳ ᾧ καὶ συνέπαθον οὐ γὰρ τὸν νῦν ἠγάπησαν αἰῶνα ἀλλὰ τὸν ὑπὲρ ἡμῶν ἀποθανόντα καὶ δι' ἡμᾶς ὑπὸ τοῦ θεοῦ ἀναστάντα.

Summary Advice

10 In his ergo state et domini exemplar sequimini, firmi in fide et immutabiles, fraternitatis amatores, diligentes invicem, in veritate sociati, mansuetudine domini alterutri praestolantes, nullum despicientes. [2]Cum possitis benefacere, nolite differre, quia eleëmosyna de morte liberat. Omnes vobis invicem subiecti estote, conversationem vestram irreprensibilem habentes in gentibus, ut ex bonis operibus vestris et vos laudem accipiatis et dominus in vobis non blasphemetur. [3]Vae autem per quem nomen domini blasphematur. Sobrietatem ergo docete omnes in qua et vos conversamini.

- **8:2** Cf. 1 Pet 4:14–16; 1 Clem 16:17; 17:1.
- **9** Although parallel to chap. 8 as stressing an example beginning with a reference to *vindication* (or "correct behavior"), chap. 9 is formally marked with its first word (*parakalō*) as the beginning of a new unit. It also plays a large role in the two-letter hypothesis, for it evidently views *Ignatius* as a martyr who has gone to his reward. The reference to *Zosimus* and *Rufus* also raises questions, for they were not earlier companions of Ignatius. See the Introduction under "Unity." After *for us* the letter is lost in all Greek mss. Eusebius preserves the entire chapter in Greek, joining to this chapter most of chap. 13 (*Hist. eccl.* 3.36.13–15).
- **9:1** A secondary theme, not explicitly requested by the Philippians, is patient endurance. The primary model for this chapter is 1 Clement 5. The athletic metaphor *strive* (cf. Phil 3:16; Gal 2:2) suits this. *Envoys* would be a rare reference to other "apostles." It may refer to missionaries in general. If the former, it designates Peter.
- **9:2** *Present age* imitates the PE, especially 2 Tim 4:10. See 5:2 above. Valens (chap. 10) is the prime example of love for this world.

but endured everything for us so that we might have
genuine existence because of him.
[2]Let us be imitators of his endurance.
If we suffer as Christians, let us praise him.
He set this example for us in person,
and we have come to put our faith in his example.

Example 2: The Martyrs

9 Therefore I appeal to all of you to obey the invitation to correct behavior and put no limit on your patience, as you witnessed with your own eyes not only in the blessed ones, Ignatius, Zosimus, and Rufus, but also in others from your community, and in Paul himself, as well as the other envoys, [2]since you are convinced that they did not strive in vain, but with confidence and honorable behavior, and that they have now reached the position they have earned, next to the master, with whom they also suffered. For they had no fondness for the present age, but for the one who died for us and was raised by God in our behalf.

Summary Advice

10 Don't yield an inch on these matters. Follow the master's example, firmly and unswervingly trusting, cherishing the community, practicing mutual affection in genuine fellowship, gently yielding to one another as the master would, looking down on no one. [2]Don't postpone opportunities for doing good, because generosity frees one from the power of death. Do not insist upon getting your way. Conduct yourselves so irreproachably among unbelievers that you will be commended for your fine deeds and you will bring no damage to the master's name. [3]Alas for those who bring disrepute to the master's name. Teach everyone the self-discipline you yourselves exhibit.

- **10** This chapter is extant only in Latin. It is riddled with references to various texts, especially Paul and 1 Peter, probably garnered from memory. Polycarp makes his final exhortation before turning to the particular case, pressing home the thesis of chap. 8.
- **10:1** *Firmly*. Cf. 1 Cor 15:58. *Cherishing*. See 1 Pet 2:17. *Gently*. Cf. 1 Cor 10:1.
- **10:2** *Generosity*. The ultimate source is Tob 4:11, possibly derived secondhand. *Insist* is from Eph 5:21. On *conduct yourselves* see 1 Pet 2:12.
- **10:3** *Alas*, lit., "woe [to any] through whom the master's name is blasphemed." This derives from Isa 52:5 through Rom 2:2; IgnTr 8:2. Polycarp does not cite the LXX directly. The issue is the community's reputation among outsiders. Cases like that of Valens bring ridicule upon the church, as in Lucian's *On the Death of Peregrinus* 13. *Self-discipline* evokes 1 Thess 4:1. The verb *teach* could be imperative or indicative. The former is preferable.

The Valens Situation

Greed

11 Nimis contristatus sum pro valente, qui presbyter factus est aliquando apud vos, quod sic ignoret is locum qui datus est ei. Moneo itaque ut abstineatis vos ab avaritia et sitis casti veraces. abstinete vos ab omni malo. [2]Qui autem non potest se in his gubernare, quomodo alii pronuntiat hoc? Si quis non se abstinuerit ab avaritia, ab idolotatria conquinabitur et tamquam inter gentes iudicabitur, qui ignorant iudicium domini. Aut nescimus, quia sancti mundum iudicabunt? sicut Paulus docet. [3]Ego autem nihil tale sensi in vobis vel audivi, in quibus laboravit beatus Paulus, qui estis in principio epistulae eius. De vobis etenim gloriatur in omnibus ecclesiis, quae dominum solae tunc cognoverant; nos autem nondum cognoveramus. [4]Valde ergo, fratres, constristor pro illo et pro coniuge eius, quibus det dominus paenitentiam veram. Sobrii ergo estote et vos in hoc; et non sicut inimicos tales existimetis, sed sicut passibilia membra et errantia eos revocate, ut omnium vestrum corpus salvetis. Hoc enim agentes vos ipsos aedificatis.

12 Confido enim vos bene exercitatos esse in sacris literis et nihil vos latet; mihi autem non est concessum. Modo, ut his scripturis dictum est, irascimini et nolite peccare, et sol non occidat super

---

11:3 The text is difficult and probably corrupt. The Latin reads "You who are at the beginning of his epistle." Many solutions have been proposed. One, already in a Latin ms, reads "church" (*ecclesiae*) instead of "letter" (*epistulae*). The phrase that follows evokes 2 Thess 1:4. M. Holmes's economical solution supplies a verb "praise" for "are." This is adopted here.

- **11** Polycarp now comes to the case of Valens, identified as a former presbyter, who had evidently misused or misappropriated funds, had been exposed, and had either been excommunicated or had abandoned the church. The bishop's pastoral orientation is on display here. Although he despises the deed, he shows concern for Valens and his wife, who had evidently departed with him. His primary concern is for the community, which has been damaged by this action. Such notions of purity are foreign to us, who presume that by denouncing misconduct we avoid association with it. To exchange alleged "superstition" for naïveté is not a good bargain. Polycarp uses Valens as a text for a general denunciation of avarice and does not return to the former presbyter until v. 4.
- **11:1** *Pure* (*casti*) is a cultic term, signaling the role of purity.
- **11:2** *How can . . . ?* Polycarp borrows from the Pastor's definition of a *bishop*, 1 Tim 3:5. *Idolatry*. The link between avarice and idolatry is traditional: Testament of Judah 19:1; Col 3:5/Eph 5:5. The rationale is that what one pursues above all else is one's god. *Judge*. 1 Cor 6:2 is the source. This leads Polycarp

The Valens Situation

11 I feel deep grief for Valens, who had once served as a *presbyter* among you, that he should have so little understanding of the office conferred upon him. This leads me to warn you to avoid greed. Be pure and truthful. Steer clear every sort of evil. [2]How can someone unable to manage himself in these matters tell others to do so? Those unduly fond of money will be treated like unbelievers defiled by idolatry and ignorant of the master's condemnation. Or are we unaware that God's people will judge everyone, as Paul teaches? [3]I have no such notion about you nor have I heard anything of the sort, you among whom the blessed Paul labored, you who are [commended] at the opening of his letter. He brags about you in all the communities he founded, those that had come to know the master when we had not. [4]Therefore, sisters and brothers, I feel deep grief for Valens and his spouse. May the master grant them to have a complete change of heart. Be prudent in this matter. Don't view such people as enemies, but as frail and errant members of the body. Restore them so that you may save your entire body. By doing this you strengthen the community.

Greed

12 I am confident that you are well educated in the sacred writings. No meaning eludes you—more than I can say for myself. Nonetheless, as it says in these scriptures: "if you get angry, do not

---

to invoke Paul's authority, to which the Philippians are no strangers. As is characteristic of the Deuteropauline tradition, Paul is primarily a pastor and teacher rather than a missionary. Polycarp's references to various letters indicate the he implicitly holds the view that what Paul wrote to one, he wrote to all. This principle is not stated explicitly until c. 200, but it justified the collection and dissemination of his letters.

- **11:4** See 2 Thess 3:15; 1 Clem 37:5; 38:1. Those treated as enemies become enemies. Polycarp views Mr. & Mrs. Valens as members of the body, rather than outcasts or exiles. This status motivates both charity and attempts to bring them back. The price of this position is a tendency to moralize the concept of the Body of Christ.
- **12** The chapter division is infelicitous, as 12:1 completes the argument of chap. 11, while v. 2 moves toward the close. As noted in the introduction, chaps. 12 and 14 are arguably modeled upon the structure displayed at the close of 1 Clement 64–65 (arguably does not mean certainly). Verse 2 ably touches upon the foregoing themes.
- **12:1** For his closing exhortation the Bishop of Smyrna turns to sacred texts. 2 Timothy 3:16 is in mind, as well as 2 Tim 1:5. The former may explain the use of two different words for "writings." Polycarp's flattery and appar-

iracundiam vestram. Beatus, qui meminerit; quod ego credo esse in vobis.

Epistolary Close

[2]Deus autem et pater domini nostri Iesu Christi, et ipse sempiternus pontifex, dei filius Iesus Christus, aedificet vos in fide et veritate et in omni mansuetudine et sine iracundia et in patientia et in longanimitate et tolerantia et castitate; et det vobis sortem et partem inter sanctos suos et nobis vobiscum et omnibus, qui sunt sub caelo, qui credituri sunt in dominum nostrum et deum Iesum Christum et in ipsius patrem, qui resuscitavit eum a mortuis. [3]Pro omnibus sanctis orate. Orate etiam pro regibus et potestatibus et principibus atque pro persequentibus et odientibus vos et pro inimicis crucis, ut fructus vester manifestus sit in omnibus, ut sitis in illo perfecti.

Personal Data (One-Letter Hypothesis)

13 Ἐγράψατέ μοι καὶ ὑμεῖς καὶ Ἰγνάτιος ἵν' ἐάν τις ἀπέρχηται εἰς Συρίαν καὶ τὰ παρ' ὑμῶν ἀποκομίσῃ γράμματα ὅπερ ποιήσω ἐὰν λάβω καιρὸν εὔθετον εἴτε ἐγώ εἴτε ὃν πέμπω πρεσβεύσοντα καὶ περὶ ὑμῶν [2]τὰς ἐπιστολὰς Ἰγνατίου τὰς πεμφθείσας ἡμῖν ὑπ' αὐτοῦ καὶ ἄλλας ὅσας εἴχομεν παρ' ἡμῖν ἐπέμψαμεν ὑμῖν καθὼς ἐνετείλασθε αἵτινες ὑποτεταγμέναι εἰσὶν τῇ ἐπιστολῇ ταύτῃ ἐξ ὧν μεγάλα ὠφεληθῆναι δυνήσεσθε περιέχουσι γὰρ πίστιν καὶ ὑπομονὴν

12:2 Some Latin witnesses read "our master and God." Although it is tempting to discard this as a later interpolation, it could be the earliest reading, lost through visual error.

---

ent false modesty intend to encourage the Philippians to make use of the resources they already have. Some may argue that the modesty is not false, as Polycarp does not exhibit his biblical literacy. Since he seems to know 1 Peter and 1 Clement by heart, his silence speaks loudly. Be that as it may, he has a passage to offer: Eph 4:26, which incorporates the first part of Ps 4:5. The usage is quite akin to 1 Tim 5:18, upon which Polycarp has modeled himself, or possibly the environment shared by both regards Pauline texts as authoritative "writings." Possibly the Philippians' request cited some texts from Paul. The closing macarism is common.

- **12:2** has two parts: a prayer for the faithful in blessing/wish form and instruction on objects of prayer. *High priest* points to Christ's intercessory role. See Hebrews (e.g. 4:14; 10:29) and 1 Clement (36:1; 61:3; 64). The verb *build* is, however, singular.
- **12:3** Prayer for rulers is common in writings seeking a place in society. See 1 Tim 2:1–2. *Enemies* derives from Phil 3:18, although the identity of those enemies has shifted.

sin," and "don't let the sun go down on your wrath." Congratulations to those who keep these sentiments in mind, as I am sure you do.

Epistolary Close

[2]May the God and parent of our master Jesus Christ, and the perpetual high priest himself, the son of God Jesus Christ, build in trust, honesty, and in all courtesy, without anger and with forbearance, consistency, patient endurance, and purity, and grant you a share and place among God's people, and to us, with you and all people under the sky who will come to believe in our master and God Jesus Christ and his father, who brought Christ back from the dead. [3]Pray for all God's people. Pray also for monarchs, magistrates and rulers, for those who hate and persecute you, for enemies of the cross, so that the result of your piety might be clear to all and that you might reach your goal in Christ.

Personal Data (One-Letter Hypothesis)

13 Both you and Ignatius wrote me that anyone going to Syria should also convey your letter. This I shall do if a suitable opportunity arises—either in person or through a representative I dispatch on behalf of you as well as myself. [2]In addition we are enclosing the letters of Ignatius that he sent us and others in our possession, as you directed. You will find them highly profitable, as they contain material dealing with trust and patience under stress and every-

---

To examine the merits of the two-letter hypothesis, turn immediately to chap. 14. Then read chaps 12–14 consecutively to view the other perspective

- **13** Eusebius (*Hist. eccl.* 3.36.14–15) preserves this text in Greek, except for the last sentence. The best explanation for this omission is that the church historian perceived that it was at variance with chap. 9, which he had just quoted. From chap. 9 readers gather that Ignatius was a martyr. 13.2 implies that news about him had not yet reached Smyrna. See the Introduction under "Unity." This brief paragraph underlines the nature of private communication in antiquity. Correspondence was sent by hand. The rich might delegate this task to a slave, but others had to wait for someone who planned to go to that destination or undertake the task personally. Chapter 13 also illustrates the interest in and means of collecting letters. See 1 Thess 5:27; Col 4:16.
- **13:1** On Ignatius' interest in Polycarp's travel, see IgnSm 11:2; Polycarp 7:2.
- **13:2** Although he happily shares Ignatius' letters, the bishop of Smyrna does not hesitate to tell his readers what they contain. One would not easily gather that Ignatius reveled in dazzling rhetoric, exhibited a vigorous theology, and viewed order as the path to unity. In short, the sentence says more about Polycarp's priorities than those of Ignatius.

καὶ πᾶσαν οἰκοδομὴν τὴν εἰς τὸν κύριον ἡμῶν ἀνήκουσαν. Et de ipso Ignatio et de his qui cum eo sunt, quod certius agnoveritis, significate.

14 Haec vobis scripsi per Crescentem, quem in praesenti commendavi vobis et nunc commendo. conversatus est enim nobiscum inculpabiliter; credo quia et vobiscum similiter. Sororem autem eius habebitis commendatam, cum venerit ad vos.

Epistolary Close, Continued

Incolumes estote in domino Iesu Christo in gratia eum omnibus vestris. Amen.

• **14** In the two-letter hypothesis this closes the longer letter. Crescens may have carried the earlier note with the Ignatian correspondence. Polycarp uses a pattern like that found in 1 Clem 63:3.

thing leading to growth in our master. As for Ignatius and his companions, please advise us if you learn anything definitive.

14 I am writing via Crescens, whom I recently recommended to you and now do so once more. His conduct while with us has been impeccable; I believe that you will have the same experience. Please consider his sister as also recommended, when she arrives.

Epistolary Close, Continued

Best wishes and divine favor to you and yours in our master Jesus Christ.

- **14:1** *Recently* implies that the Latin *in praesenti* ("at present") poorly renders a Greek word that can mean "recently." *Crescens* was the letter carrier. By commending him Polycarp suggests that he is a reliable source of information. See Rom 16:1–2; 1 Cor 16:15–16; Phil 2:25–30; Col 4:7–8. The name is Latin.

WORKS CONSULTED

Aageson, James W. *Paul, the Pastoral Epistles, and the Early Church.* Peabody, MA: Hendrickson, 2008.

Akurgal, Ekrem. *Ancient Civilizations and Ruins of Turkey.* 8th ed. Trans. M. Emre and J. Whybrow. Istanbul: Güzel Sanatlar Matbaasi, 1993.

Bakirtis, Charalambos, and Helmut Koester, eds. *Philippi at the Time of Paul and after His Death.* Harrisburg, PA: Trinity International, 1998.

Barnard, L. W. "The Problem of St. Polycarp's Epistle to the Philippians." Pp. 31–39 in *Studies in the Apostolic Fathers and Their Background.* New York: Schocken, 1966.

Barnett, Albert E. *Paul Becomes a Literary Influence.* Chicago: University of Chicago Press, 1941.

Bartlet, J. V., et al. *The New Testament in the Apostolic Fathers.* Oxford: Clarendon Press, 1905.

Bauer, Johannes Bapt. *Die Polykarpbriefe. KAV.* Göttingen: Vandenhoeck & Ruprecht, 1995.

Bauer, Walter, and Henning Paulsen. *Die Briefe des Ignatius von Antiochia und der Polykarpbrief.* HNT 18. Tübingen: Mohr Siebeck, 1985.

Bernard, J. H. *The Pastoral Epistles.* Cambridge: Cambridge University Press, 1899.

Bormann, Lukas. *Philippi: Stadt und Christengemeinde zur Zeit des Paulus.* NovTSup 79. Leiden: Brill, 1995.

Cadoux, Cecil J. *Ancient Smyrna: A History of the City from the Earliest Times to 324 A.D.* Oxford: Basil Blackwell, 1938.

Campenhausen, Hans v. "Polykarp von Smyrna und die Pastoralbriefe." Pp. 197–252 of *Aus der Frühzeit des Christentums.* Tübingen: Mohr Siebeck, 1963.

Dehandschutter, Boudewijn. "The Epistle of Polycarp." Pp. 117–33 in *The Apostolic Fathers: An Introduction.* Ed. William Pratscher. Waco, TX: Baylor University Press, 2010.

Dewey, Joanna. "1 Timothy–Titus." Pp. 595–604 in *Women's Bible Commentary.* Ed. Carol A. Newsome et al. 3rd ed. Louisville: Westminster John Knox, 2012.

Dibelius, Martin, and Hans Conzelmann. *The Pastoral Epistles.* Hermeneia. Trans. Phillip Buttolph and Adela Yarbro. Philadelphia: Fortress Press, 1972.

Easton, Burton Scott. *The Pastoral Epistles.* New York: Scribner, 1947.

Fiore, Benjamin, S. J. *The Pastoral Epistles: First Timothy, Second Timothy, Titus. SacPag*. Collegeville, MN: Liturgical Press, 2007.

Glaser, Timo. *Paulus als Briefroman erzählt: Studien zum antiken Briefroman und seiner christlichen Rezeption in den Pastoralbriefen*. NTOA 76. Göttingen: Vandenhoeck & Ruprecht, 2009.

Harrison, P. N. *Paulines and Pastorals*. London: Villiers, 1964.

____. *Polycarp's Two Epistles to the Philippians*. Cambridge: The University Press, 1936.

____. *The Problem of the Pastoral Epistles*. Oxford: OUP Humphrey Milford, 1921.

Hartog, Paul. *Polycarp's* Epistle to the Philippians *and the* Martyrdom of Polycarp: *Introduction, Text, and Commentary*. Oxford Apostolic Fathers. Oxford: Oxford University Press, 2013.

Hendrix, Holly. "Philippi." Pp. 313–17 in *Anchor Bible Dictionary*. Ed. David Noel Freedman. Vol. 5. 8th ed. New Haven: Yale University Press, 1992.

Holmes, Michael. "Polycarp of Smyrna, *Epistle to the Philippians*." Pp. 108–25 in *The Writings of the Apostolic Fathers*. Ed. Paul Foster. London: T&T Clark, 2007.

Holzberg, Niklas, ed. *Der griechische Briefroman: Gattungstypologie und Textanalyse*. Classica Monacensia 8. Tübingen: Gunter Narr, 1994.

____. "Letters: *Chion*." Pp. 645–53 in *The Novel in the Ancient World*. Ed. Gareth Schmeling. Rev. ed. Leiden: Brill, 2003.

Hultgren, Arland J. *I-II Timothy, Titus*. ACNT. Minneapolis: Augsburg Press, 1984.

Jefford, Clayton N. *Reading the Apostolic Fathers: An Introduction*. Peabody, MA: Baker Academic, 1996.

Johnson, Luke Timothy. *The First and Second Letters to Timothy*. Anchor Bible. New York: Doubleday, 2001.

Kleist, James A. *Didache, Barnabas, Polycarp, Papias, Diognetus*. ACW 6. Westminster, MD: Newman, 1948.

Koester, Helmut, ed. *Ephesos: Metropolis of Asia*. HTS 41 Valley Forge: Trinity Press International, 1995.

____. "Ephesos in Early Christian Literature." Pp. 119–40 in Koester, *Ephesos*.

Koukouli-Chrysantaki, Chaido. "Colonia Iulia Augusta Philippensis." Pp. 5–35 in *Philippi at the Time of Paul and After His Death*. Eds. Helmut Koester and Charalambos Bakirtzis. Valley Forge: Trinity Press International, 1998.

Lightfoot, Joseph Barber. *The Apostolic Fathers*. 2d ed. 2 Parts in 5 vols. Grand Rapids: Baker, 1989 (reprint of 1889–90), "Introduction to Polycarp," 2:1:433–727.

Lock, Walter. *The Pastoral Epistles*. ICC. Edinburgh: T&T Clark, 1924.

MacDonald, Dennis R. *The Legend and the Apostle: The Battle for Paul in Story and*

Canon. Philadelphia: Westminster Press, 1983.

Malherbe, Abraham. *The Cynic Epistles*. SBLSBS 12. Missoula, Montana: Scholars Press, 1977.

Maloney, Linda M. "The Pastoral Epistles." Pp. 361–80 in *Searching the Scriptures*. Vol. 2. *A Feminist Commentary*. Ed. Elisabeth Schüssler Fiorenza. New York: Crossroad Publishing Co., 1994.

Marshall, I. H. *The Pastoral Epistles*. ICC. Edinburgh: T&T Clark, 1999.

Mertz, Annette. *Die Fiktive Selbstauslegung des Paulus. Intertextuelle Studien zur Intention und Reception der Pastoralbriefe*. NTOA 52. Göttingen: Vandenhoeck & Ruprecht, 2004.

Mounce, William. D. *The Pastoral Epistles*. WBC 46. Nashville: Nelson, 2000.

Nielsen, Charles M. "Polycarp, Paul, and the Scriptures." *ATR* 47 (1965) 199–216.

Norden, Eduard. *Die antike Kunstprosa*. 2 vols. Stuttgart: Teubner, 1995.

O'Connor, Jerome Murphy. *St. Paul's Ephesus. Texts and Archaeology*. Collegeville, MN: Liturgical Press, 2008.

Paulsen, Hennig. *Die Briefe des Ignatius von Antiochia und der Brief des Polykarp von Smyrna*. A revision of W. Bauer. HNT 18. Tübingen: Mohr Siebeck, 1985.

Pervo, Richard. *Acts: A Commentary*. Ed. Harold Attridge. Hermeneia. Minneapolis: Fortress Press, 2009.

____. "Acts in Ephesus (and Environs) c. 115." *Forum* 3d Series 4 (2015) 125–51.

____. *The Making of Paul: Constructions of the Apostle in Early Christianity*. Minneapolis: Fortress Press, 2010.

____. "Romancing an Oft-neglected Stone: The Pastoral Epistles and the Epistolary Novel." *Journal of Higher Criticism* 1 (1994) 25–47.

Pilhofer, Peter. *Philippi: Die erste christlih = che Gemeinde Europas*. WUNT 87. Tübingen: Mohr Siebeck, 1995.

Potter, D. S. "Smyrna." Pp. 73–75 in *Anchor Bible Dictionary*. Ed. David Noel Freedman. Vol. 6. 8th ed. New Haven: Yale University Press, 1992.

Rensberger, David K. "As the Apostle Teaches: The Development of the Use of Paul's Letters in Second-Century Christianity." PhD. diss. Yale, 1981.

Rothschild, Clare K. *Paul in Athens*. WUNT 341. Tübingen: Mohr Siebeck, 2014.

Schoedel, William R. *Polycarp, Martyrdom of Polycarp, Fragments of Papias. The Apostolic Fathers. A New Translation and Commentary*. Ed. R.M. Grant. Vol. 5. Camden, NJ: Nelson, 1967.

____. "Polycarp of Smyrna and Ignatius of Antioch." *ANRW* 2.27.1 (1993) 272–358.

Spicq, Ceslas. *Theological Lexicon of the New Testament*. 3 vols. Trans. and ed. J. D. Ernest. Peabody, MA: Hendrickson, 1994.

Streete, Gail Corrington. "Askesis and Resistance in the Pastoral Letters." Pp. 299–316 in *Asceticims and the New Testament*. Eds. Lief Vaage and V. L. Wimbush. London: Routledge, 1999.

Towner, Philip H. *The Pastoral Epistles*. NICNT. Grand Rapids: Eerdmans, 2000.

Trebilco, Paul R. *The Early Christians in Ephesus from Paul to Ignatius*. WUNT 166. Tübingen: Mohr Siebeck, 2004.

Turner, Nigel. *Style*. Vol. 4 of *A Grammar of New Testament Greek*. Ed. James Hope Moulton. Edinburgh: T&T Clark, 1976.

Young, Frances. *The Theology of the Pastoral Letters*. Cambridge: Cambridge University Press, 1994.

INDEX OF ANCIENT SOURCES

ABOUT THE AUTHOR

Richard I. Pervo earned a Th.D. at Harvard University and taught at Seabury-Western Theological Seminary and at the University of Minnesota in Minneapolis. A specialist in narratives about apostles and in the Pauline legacy, he is the author of many books, most recently *The Acts of John* (Early Christian Apocrypha, 2015), and *The Acts of Paul: A New Translation with Introduction and Commentary* (2014).

ALSO BY RICHARD PERVO

The Acts of John (Early Christian Apocrypha, 2015)

The Acts of Paul: A New Translation with Introduction and Commentary (2014)

The Gospel of Luke (Scholars Bible, 2014)

The Making of Paul: Constructions of the Apostle in Early Christianity (2010)

Acts: A Commentary. (Hermeneia, 2009)

The Mystery of Acts (2008)

Dating Acts: Between the Evangelists and the Apologists (2006)

Rethinking the Unity of Luke and Acts (with M. Parsons, 1993)

Luke's Story of Paul (1990)

Profit with Delight: The Literary Genre of the Acts of the Apostles (1987)

www.ingramcontent.com/pod-product-compliance
Lightning Source LLC
Chambersburg PA
CBHW060403090426
42734CB00011B/2242

* 9 7 8 1 5 9 8 1 5 1 7 8 7 *